Praise for Running Doc™, Lewis G. Maharam, MD

"Dr. Maharam is at the forefront of exercise-related medical issues in the U.S. and around the world. In his work as a marathon medical director, he has done much to make the sport of distance running safer and more enjoyable for hundreds of thousands of runners. He's that rare sports medicine expert who knows how to explain the science in terms that average athletes can understand and follow."

—Amby Burfoot, former executive editor of Runner's World *magazine*

"Running Doc is the most knowledgeable and articulate medical professional in the running industry. His willingness to share his expertise has prevented countless medical emergencies and personal hardships. More than that, his warmth and humor ease the anxiety of those with whom he speaks."

—John "The Penguin" Bingham, columnist for Competitor *magazine*

"When runners get hurt, they fly to Dr. Maharam!"

—Meb Keflezighi, 2009 New York City Marathon winner and 2004 Olympic silver medalist

"Running Doc brings a unique blend of anecdotal experience and medical science to the sports world, particularly distance running. He knows how to keep people exercising safely. Best of all, he can do it by explaining things in a way that everyone can understand."

—Frank Shorter, 1972 Olympic marathon gold medalist and 1976 Olympic marathon silver medalist

"Dr. Maharam is the definitive medical resource for the running and walking industry. His brilliance is in the delivery. He entertains as he educates, leaving you with great information and a smile on your face."

—Jenny Hadfield, running coach and columnist for Runner's World *and* Health *magazines and author of* Running for Mortals

"Dr. Maharam is the premier running doctor in the world! He has carved out a specific medical specialty for taking care of runners. I was lucky to have him formulate our medical plans and lead our medical teams as well as educate our runners. This book will be an invaluable resource for all runners at all levels."

—Allan Steinfeld, former president and CEO of New York Road Runners and race director of the New York City Marathon

"If you've got a sports injury, Dr. Maharam is the go-to doctor, and his book is the go-to resource for patients and doctors."

—Steven Van Camp, MD, FACSM, former president of
the American College of Sports Medicine

"It didn't take long to realize that Maharam was the best student I ever had. He absorbed everything we knew about the biomechanics of running and walking. He has gone on to become an expert in the physiology of running. I have enjoyed watching him become the best and [am proud] that I was able to help him accomplish that."

—Allan M. Levy, MD, former team physician of the New York Giants,
the New Jersey Nets, and the New York Islanders

"Dr. Maharam is innovative, dedicated, and great both behind the scenes making it happen as well as front and center speaking to a group. He stays current and informed. Dr. Maharam is sure to make you think and stimulate discussion on any topic he covers."

—Heidi Skolnik, MS, CDN, FACSM, contributing advisor to
Men's Health magazine and former team nutritionist of
the New York Giants and the New York Mets

"Dr. Maharam, Running Doc, has been my medical director for some 25 years. We entrust the health and safety of 400,000 participants in the Rock 'n' Roll Marathon Series each year to his care. He is far and away the best and most experienced doctor specializing in running and marathon medicine in the world, and I would hate to ever have to put on an event of any size without his guidance and oversight. Perhaps even more important, though, I would send anyone whom I cared about with any ailment to see him. He is the best diagnostician I have ever known. He understands the medical side of the sport like no one else. He 'connects the dots' like Picasso and is able to communicate all manner of medical complexities in terms that we laymen can understand. This will be the definitive book on running injuries."

—Tracy Sundlun, senior vice president for events of the Competitor Group,
cofounder of the Rock 'n' Roll Marathon Series,
and former Olympic track coach

Running Doc's™
Guide to Healthy Running

Running Doc's™ Guide to Healthy Running

How to Fix Injuries, Stay Active, and Run Pain-Free

Lewis G. Maharam, MD, FACSM

BOULDER, COLORADO

3002 Sterling Circle, Suite 100
Boulder, Colorado 80301 USA
(303) 440-0601 · Fax (303) 444-6788 · E-mail velopress@competitorgroup.com

Distributed in the United States and Canada by Ingram Publisher Services.

Library of Congress Cataloging-in-Publication Data
Maharam, Lewis G.
Running doc's guide to healthy running: how to fix injuries, stay active, and run pain-free / **Lewis G. Maharam.**
    p.   cm.
  Includes index.
  ISBN 978-1-934030-68-4 (pbk.: alk. paper)
  1. Running—Training.   2. Sports injuries.   I. Title.
GV1061.5.M24 2011
796.42—dc22
2010053416

For information on purchasing VeloPress books, please call (800) 811-4210 ext. 2138
or visit www.velopress.com.

Cover illustration and design and interior illustrations by Charlie Layton
Interior design by Erin Johnson Design
Composition by Chris Davis, Mulberry Tree Enterprises
Text set in Charlotte Book

11   12   13   /   10   9   8   7   6   5   4   3   2

To Welabucs, who knew . . .

Contents

Foreword

By Frank Shorter

Dr. Lewis Maharam quite simply loves what he does. It is obvious he has always wanted to be a sports medicine physician. You can see it in the way his eyes light up whenever he describes his ongoing efforts to safeguard the health of thousands of runners, a task he assumes regularly as the medical director for major road races all around the United States.

When on site, Dr. Maharam—Rock Doc, we call him, for his role with the Rock 'n' Roll Marathon Series—is constantly fine-tuning his protocols, adding new ideas to the way he organizes his field hospital and medical aid stations along a race route, and seeking to innovate his approaches to better care. His attention to detail and his practical methods of advising and treating runners, combined with his common sense, make him uniquely qualified to write about the medical side of running. For runners, it's all about persevering and moving on down the road. The Rock Doc has the tools and wisdom to help us all do that.

Several years ago, when we were on stage together to lead a clinic at a Rock 'n' Roll Marathon expo, I finished answering a question from the audience, and the Doc turned to me. He whispered, "I am incredibly impressed by how some elite athletes like you intuitively know the right thing to do with regard to training and injuries." I was flattered, but it also made me realize that a big part of Dr. Maharam's role lies in interpreting and spreading the knowledge he gathers and in making sure that those athletes who are not able to listen to their bodies quite as well are still able to maximize their chances of success by following his guidelines.

You may be surprised by the tone of this book. This is not a dry, clinical presentation. It is not a simple glossary of medical conditions and treatments either—although, make no mistake, the aches, pains, and injuries that we runners get are fully described and explained, along with the Doc's recommended treatments. But in this book he also draws on many personal stories from his vast experience in his medical practice in New York City and from the cases he sees in the field. He uses these stories to show how he diagnoses and treats his patients. It's like having a personal doctor who is also a good friend sit down at your side and explain what's going on and what to do. Dr. Maharam's advice on preventive measures is concise, and the way he presents it is easy to remember.

Running injuries can be complicated, but even in sports medicine, the simplest explanation and suggested treatment often produce the best result. Here is a doctor who can provide you with the questions you should ask your own provider in an effort to stay active and injury-free.

Whenever runners get together, we like to talk about our training, our recent races, and, invariably, our injuries. If your goal is to stay as active as possible for as long as you can, I can think of no better book to read and keep close by for future reference.

Frank Shorter ignited the first American running boom in the 1970s when he won the gold medal in the marathon at the 1972 Olympics. He also won the silver medal in the marathon at the 1976 Olympics. In addition to his preeminence at the marathon distance, Shorter was a four-time U.S. national 10,000-meter champion and won 24 national running titles during his career. A graduate of Yale University and the University of Florida College of Law, Shorter helped to create the U.S. Anti-Doping Agency and served as its chairman from 2000 to 2003. He was elected to the U.S. Olympic Hall of Fame in 1984.

Preface

They call me Doc. Running Doc. The name fits because I am the medical director of the Rock 'n' Roll Marathon Series around the country, currently 19 races and counting. I was also the medical director of the New York Road Runners and the ING New York City Marathon for many years. I am now responsible for more than half a million racers a year in addition to my private practice in New York City.

I am honored to be the medical director of the largest marathon and half-marathon series in the world. My work with these races has earned me another nickname: Rock Doc. That name fits, too, because there is a rock-and-roll band at each mile along the course of these events and a big concert after the race. Music has been in my soul since I was young. As a teenager, I played rhythm guitar in a rock-and-roll band. Now music and sports medicine have come together for me at these events. I am also responsible for the medical care at the Carlsbad 5000 (the world's fastest 5K race) in California, and I am at the finish-line medical tents supervising the care for all these racers nationwide.

The practice of sports medicine means more to me than anything else. I treat runners, walkers, and other endurance athletes from around the globe as well as all sports injuries. Helping these people stay healthy and happy, no matter what their goals, has become my life's work.

This book is written for everyone who is currently a runner or walker and anyone who aspires to take part in these sports, at any level and at any distance. Although much of the advice is about taking part in road races, you will learn a great deal even if you have no plans to join in a race. (And by the way, if you've never run or walked in a race, what are you waiting for? These events cater to runners and walkers at all levels, and they are a great way to set a goal, have fun, meet people, travel, and raise funds for worthy causes.) Whether you are an experienced athlete or a beginner, you will undergo physical and mental changes during endurance training and competing.

This book will help you understand, manage, and appreciate these changes, and it will guide you over the inevitable bumps in the road.

Successful participation comes down to understanding what is going on with your body. This includes knowing how best to work with physical changes and make the most of them to push your body far enough to make a difference and enable you to relish the challenge, but not so far as to risk overstress or injury. With proper advice, this should all be a positive life-changing experience—and fun!

My hope is that this book will answer some simple questions for you about training, planning, and medical issues and will also point you in the right direction when medical care is necessary. Most of all I hope that it will help you keep running, stay healthy, and enjoy every minute of your running career. Here's to healthy running and many enjoyable miles to come.

Acknowledgments

Writing this book has been a dream of mine since I first started to practice sports medicine. I need to acknowledge and thank:

My book agent Jack, whose expertise and encouragement made this project happen.

The extraordinary group at VeloPress and Competitor Group, including Ted, Kara, Andy, Tracy, Scott, Peter, Rebecca, Mario, and all the staff that make the writing of this book, the preparation of my columns for the Competitor Web site and magazine, and my job as medical director of the Rock 'n' Roll events an absolute pleasure.

All the physicians and teachers in my training who have helped mold the way I think and treat patients daily, including Mrs. Vovis and Drs. Majumdar, Hurst, Walker, Levy, and McNerney.

My friend Eddie Brill, who encouraged me to write as I speak, with humor and enthusiasm.

My family growing up: Papa Eddie (Welabucs), Grandmother Bebe, Mother Jane, and Sister Patsy. Their love and support were invaluable in the formation of who I have become.

My amazing son Eddy, the next generation sports doctor! He has been at my side as "Doctor Eddy" since he first learned to walk. Now, upon the publication of this book, he will be a third-year medical student. Every day he makes me more proud of the gentleman he has turned out to be. I love you, my son.

My wife, Amy, whom it took me 52 years to find! I love her more every day I am with her! Her daily loving enthusiasm makes the ride even more enjoyable.

And last but not least, my patients and participants in all the events I cover. Every day is interesting and fun. I get no greater joy than seeing athletes conquer their injuries and conditions and go back to play their sport pain-free.

—*Lewis G. Maharam, MD, FACSM, aka Running Doc*

DEFINITIONS

Definitions

Doctors speak their own language. In med school, absorbing all the different terms for body parts, health conditions, and medical procedures was like learning a foreign language. But in medical practice, of course, knowing the lingo cold is absolutely necessary; calling something a "thingy-dingy" just doesn't work when one doctor is speaking to another in consultation.

However, at times when speaking to patients, I have found myself slipping in a medical term that my patient doesn't understand or I find that my patient misunderstands the difference, say, between a muscle strain and a ligament sprain. In this section, therefore, I want to place us on the same page regarding the medical references you may hear in a doctor's office. Please do not be insulted if I seem to have oversimplified the definitions; if you feel that way, I apologize. My intention is for all of us to understand what we are talking about in the simplest possible way. Indeed, in many cases there really is no need to get technical when a quick definition will do the trick.

Abrasion: A scrape.

Acute injury: An injury that just happened and about which the patient can pinpoint something he or she did at a specific point in time and had immediate pain when doing it. This is the *inflection point*[1] of the injury (the exact point at which the injury occurred). Cf. *chronic condition*.

Anterior: Toward the front of the body. Cf. *posterior*. See also *lateral*, *medial*.

Arrhythmia: An irregular or abnormal heartbeat.

---

[1] Words in italics have their own definitions.

Arthroscopy: Microscopic surgery through an arthroscope, which is an instrument for viewing the interior of a joint, such as the knee. The advantages of arthroscopic surgery over traditional open surgery are that the incision is small and recovery is quick.

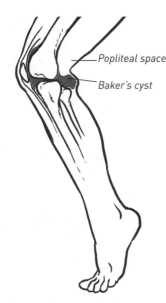

Popliteal space

Baker's cyst

Figure D.1

Baker's cyst

Baker's cyst (sometimes called a popliteal cyst because it is found in the *popliteal space* or *popliteal fossa*): A knee *effusion*. In a closed knee joint space, the weakest point is the back of the knee. When the knee is injured and fluid builds up, the back of the knee pushes outward and takes on the appearance of a cyst, which is why this condition is (incorrectly) called a Baker's cyst, although it is not a cyst. Fix what is wrong inside the knee, the fluid stops being produced, and this swelling goes away. Surgeries to remove the "cyst" are usually unsuccessful because the underlying problem that is causing the fluid buildup, such as a torn meniscus, is not addressed.

Bone: A hard white structure that gives the body form and protects the internal organs. Bones are made up of calcium, phosphorus, sodium, and other minerals, including the protein collagen. The soft centers of the bones (the marrow), especially in the bigger bones, make blood cells.

There are 206 bones in the human body, or 208 if the sternum is counted as 3 bones. Figures D.2 and D.3 contain only the principal bones and the bone groups most likely to be discussed in patient consultations with a doctor.

Bursa: A fluid-filled sac between a muscle or a tendon and a bone that provides a cushion between the parts. The bursa reduces friction and allows the tendon or muscle to move freely.

Bursitis: An inflamed bursa.

Cartilage: A smooth material lining of the *bones* that allows the bones to move smoothly over one another. The blood supply to cartilage is not the best, and cartilage does not usually heal well when torn.

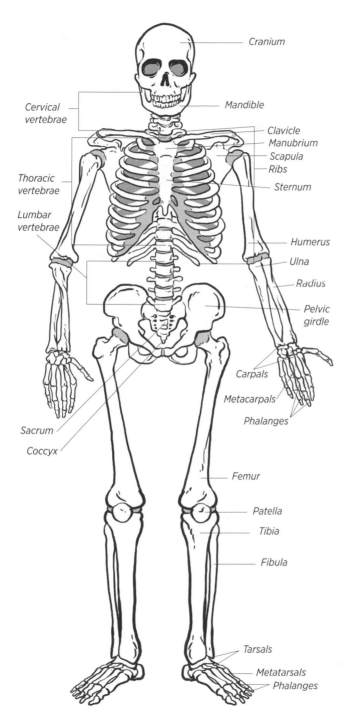

Figure D.2

The human skeleton, front view

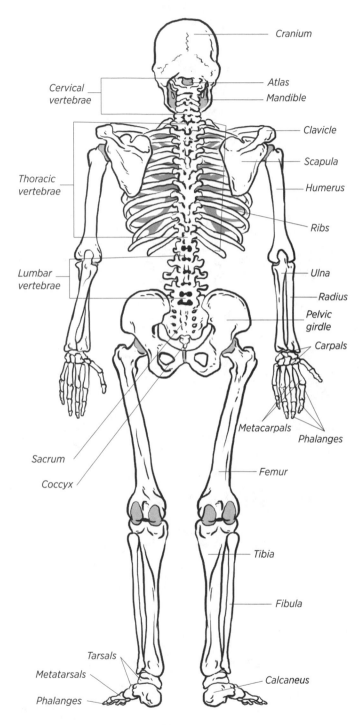

Figure D.3

The human skeleton, rear view

When *arthroscopy* is performed, the cartilage is usually cut like a linoleum tile, just as we did in art class in elementary school. When the tear is scooped out, the structure is restored, relieving pain and allowing easy movement again.

Chronic condition: An injury or condition, sometimes called an overuse injury, that occurred over time and about which a patient reports that it happened sometime after an activity. In fact, this problem most probably occurred over more than that one activity and is due to a biomechanical flaw that stressed a *bone* or soft tissue over some period of time.

The best way to understand a chronic condition is to think of a pair of corduroy pants. If you are sitting and scratching the corduroy, over time you will scratch a hole through the fabric. In this case, however, the hole is *tendinitis* or a *stress syndrome*. Cf. *acute injury*.

Contusion: A bruise. Contusions turn black and blue due to the breaking of blood vessels and the released blood subsequently drying. With time, more colors arise, like Joseph's Technicolor Dreamcoat. All of this is normal. For the first 72 hours, use only ice so as not to allow heat to further damage blood vessel walls. After 72 hours, use warm soaks to help the body absorb the dried blood.

CT scan, or computerized tomography: A technique that uses a computer to combine a series of cross-sectional X-rays into a three-dimensional image. Also called CAT scan, for computerized axial tomography.

Dorsiflexion: Bending a body part backward toward the *extensor mechanism*. For example, picking your big toe upward with your foot following the toe is dorsiflexion. Cf. *plantar flexion*.

Edema: An abnormal accumulation of fluid, often characterized by swelling.

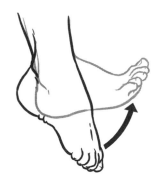

Figure D.4
Dorsiflexion

Effusion: Fluid within the closed space of a joint. Effusion can make the joint feel stiff if fluid builds up and the soft tissue forming the joint space doesn't allow the fluid to go anywhere. Effusions are a sign that something is going on within the joint that is weeping fluid, and the underlying cause (a *cartilage* or *ligament* tear or even arthritis) must be found if the effusion is to be stopped. If the effusion becomes so large that the stiffness is uncomfortable, a doctor may drain the joint; if not, that effusion fluid will naturally be absorbed and the swelling will go down with the repair of the underlying cause.

Electrolytes: Free ions found in sodium, potassium, calcium, magnesium, and so on that help regulate hydration in the body, maintain proper blood pH, and contribute to nerve and muscle function. Sports drinks that contain electrolytes can help keep salt levels balanced during extended exercise.

Extensor mechanism: A muscle or muscle group that extends or straightens a limb or body part.

Fascia: A fibrous connective tissue in the body located between the skin and *muscle*.

Fracture: A break of a *bone*.

Glycogen: The storage form of glucose. Made by the liver and muscles, glycogen acts as an energy reserve to supply the muscles with glucose to use as fuel.

Herniated disc: Pressure on a *spinal disc* that causes it to bulge; the *ligament* that holds the interior, jellylike substance of the disc to break; and that substance to leak out like a finger projection to irritate the sciatic nerve.

Inflection point: The exact moment at which an injury occurs. Pinpointing the inflection point of an injury can often help a doctor with diagnosis. See also *acute injury*.

Ischemic area: A localized area of decreased blood flow.

Joint: A place of contact where two *bones* come together. Joints are constructed to allow for movement.

Laceration: A cut.

Lateral: Toward the outside of the body. Cf. *medial*. See also *anterior*, *posterior*.

Ligament: A tissue that connects *bone* to bone.

Marathon sniffles: A cold that occurs around the time of an event due to decreased immunity.

Medial: Toward the middle of the body. Cf. *lateral*. See also *anterior*, *posterior*.

MRI, or magnetic resonance imaging: An effective and noninvasive way of taking images of the interior of the body through the use of magnets, not radiation (as with X-rays).

Muscle: A tissue that produces movement when it contracts. The contraction makes *bones* move. There are anywhere between 639 and 850 muscles in the human body, depending on who is doing the counting.

Muscle strain (also called muscle tear or pull): A tear in the *muscle's* micro- or macrostructure resulting in pain and bleeding. Severity varies, as do healing time and treatment.

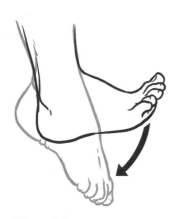

Figure D.5
Plantar flexion

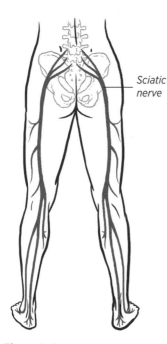

Sciatic nerve

Figure D.6
Sciatica

NSAID: A nonsteroidal anti-inflammatory drug (such as Advil, Aleve, aspirin, ibuprofen, Motrin, or naproxen).

Orthotic: An arch support device used to alter foot function and thus correct a biomechanical disorder. For running, nearly all orthotics consist of devices placed in the shoes. Orthotics can consist of simple products such as insoles or heel cups, but where serious biomechanical issues such as *overpronation* exist, a custom device specifically made for the individual is usually necessary. Custom orthotics are made from an impression of the foot and may range in length from a small heel wedge to a device that runs the full length of the foot.

Overpronation: An exaggerated *pronation* of the foot. It may be the cause of biomechanical *chronic condition*s of the foot and leg by making structures pull off the biomechanical line they were intended to follow. See also *supination*.

Overuse chronic condition: See *chronic condition*.

Plantar flexion: Bending the foot forward. For example, pushing your foot downward on the gas pedal in your car is plantar flexion. Cf. *dorsiflexion*.

Popliteal space/popliteal fossa: The area behind the knee. A "fossa" is simply a space, groove, or depression in the body.

Posterior: Toward the back of the body. Cf. *medial*. See also *anterior*, *posterior*.

Postural hypotension: Rapid decrease in blood pressure when moving from a prone position (lying down) to sitting up or standing up.

Pronation: A foot rolling inward during push-off. This is a natural, normal movement. Cf. *supination*. See also *overpronation*.

Remodeling: A breakdown and reforming of a body structure through tissue regeneration (replacing old cells with new cells). Remodeling takes place at different rates, depending on the body part. For example, the cornea remodels in 24 hours, whereas the Achilles tendon may require 3 months to completely remodel.

Sciatic nerve: The nerve that runs down the back of each leg. It is formed from the spinal nerves.

Sciatica: Pain, numbness, or tingling that travels down the leg. It arises from irritation of the *sciatic nerve* and can be caused by such conditions as *herniated discs*, degenerative discs, spinal stenosis, muscle injuries, spasm, and piriformis syndrome. If you have been said to have sciatica or suspect you have it, please see Part IV for more information, remembering that sciatica is *not* a diagnosis; it is a symptom of some other malady that must be discovered and treated.

Spinal disc: A cushy structure between spinal vertebrae whose interior is a jellylike substance and that functions as a shock absorber between the vertebrae. See also *herniated disc*.

Sprain: A tear in a *ligament*, which results in pain and swelling with black and blue discoloration. Severe tears may need surgery.

Stress fracture: A partial, ongoing fracture of a *bone* (like the cracked eggshell of a hard-boiled egg) caused by a continuum of stress adding up over time and left unaddressed. See also *stress syndrome*.

Stress syndrome: Ongoing stress to a *bone* caused by overuse or a biomechanical flaw. (On *MRI*, stress syndrome has the characteristic appearance of bone *edema*.) Without treatment, a *stress fracture* may result.

Subluxation: A partial dislocation of a *bone* from a *joint*.

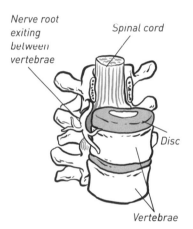

Nerve root exiting between vertebrae

Spinal cord

Disc

Vertebrae

Figure D.7A

Spinal disc, normal

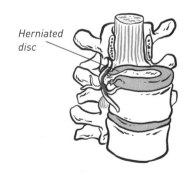

Herniated disc

Figure D.7B

Spinal disc, herniated

Supination: A foot rolling outward during push-off. This is an abnormal biomechanical motion and will lead to chronic overuse injuries. Cf. *pronation*. See also *overpronation*.

Tendinitis: Inflammation of a *tendon* caused by the tendon either rubbing on a bony surface over and over or pulling off a biomechanically optimal line. This condition is painful and needs treatment. See also *tendinosis*.

Tendinosis: The *remodeling* of an inflamed *tendon* in which, rather than lining up in parallel, the microscopic fibers of the tendon line up every which way and lead to a swollen, weak, painful tendon with an increased risk of tear. See also *tendinitis*.

Tendon: Connective tissue that attaches *muscle* to *bone*. The tendon gets its strength and flexibility by its fibers lining up in parallel. When a muscle contracts (and hence gets smaller), the tendon pulls on the bone and effects a movement. See also *tendinitis*, *tendinosis*.

Valgus: Angled outward. Cf. *varus*.

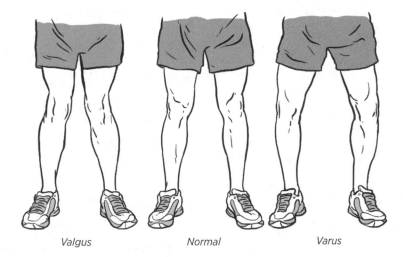

Valgus   *Normal*   *Varus*

Figure D.8

Valgus, varus

Varus: Angled inward. Cf. *valgus*.

Vertebra: A *bone* of the spine. (The plural is vertebrae.) The vertebrae collectively form the spinal column and enclose the spinal cord.

PART I
RUNNING FOR HEALTH

Running for Health

Why Run or Walk for Endurance?

Unless you have made it a point to read absolutely no health-related articles whatsoever for, say, the last 30 years, your decision to become an active, exercising person ought to be a no-brainer. We all know the health benefits of exercise and could probably tick off many of them in our sleep. And we may also know that the greatest health benefit comes when we go from being nonactive (what I call a "sofa spud") to being active, with "active" medically defined as engaging in 30 minutes of exercise five days a week.

Now, if 30 minutes a day will do the trick, then why do doctors like me recommend running or walking long distances for endurance? That's easy: because *more* is better. The heart is a muscle, and it can be trained just as well as, say, a bicep muscle in your arm. And a more efficient heart muscle makes activities of daily living more fun and less stressful. Not to mention probably keeping you around for a lot longer to enjoy that fun and reduced stress.

Walking and running are the easiest sports to fit into your life. All you need is a good pair of running or walking shoes, and you're off. And today, with more and more endurance events pouring through the cities and snaking around the countrysides of this nation, you have even more reason to get started. The next event party is waiting for you to finish your training.

Exercise indeed improves health (by reducing disease risk factors) and general well-being (by keeping the body flexible and strong to ward off the effects of aging). The benefits associated with regular exercise and physical activity contribute to a more healthy, independent lifestyle. This certainly improves the quality of life as you age.

The greatest obstacle to maintaining an exercise program is getting through the first few weeks of it. That's generally how long it takes to begin achieving an exercise high, or mood elevation, with every workout. Even if that wonderful mellowness is so subtle you hardly notice it, and even if (as some claim) it's really just a sign of a psychological addiction, it stands to reason that feeling a little euphoric after a workout gives you a solid reason to plan the next one.

You'll want to stick with your exercise program to get over the first few weeks until that subtle feeling of well-being becomes natural. But you may end up loving your program so much, like some really neat game you can play all by yourself, that you'll continue to build the length of your sessions until you're ready for marathon day!

The Benefits of Exercise

- Exercise reduces risk factors associated with disease (heart disease, high blood pressure, diabetes), which improves health status and contributes to a greater life expectancy.
- Exercise in aging adults has psychological benefits, including improved cognitive function, alleviation of depression symptoms and behavior, and improved sense of personal control and self-efficiency. (OK, you're not old yet? Well, with luck you will be someday, so it is best to start building a strong foundation now.)
- Strength training accomplished through crosstraining in addition to running helps offset the loss in muscle mass and strength typically associated with normal aging.
- Endurance training can help maintain and improve cardiac function. The heart is a muscle. It can become more efficient if trained and toned.
- Weight-bearing exercise improves bone health, thereby reducing the risk of osteoporosis. As a result, active aging adults experience fewer broken bones.
- Running regularly improves postural stability, thereby reducing the risk of falling and associated injuries and fractures.

Endurance Physiology 101

To help you understand the basics of your body's changes during endurance exercise, let's begin with a brief physiology lesson. Please don't get nervous. I know that the mere mention of "physiology" can be as intimidating for adults today as it was when we were first confronted with it in tenth-grade biology. I had the same feelings in tenth grade, but thanks to an amazing biology teacher, Mrs. Vovis, my attitude toward this subject changed. Mrs. Vovis taught us that to avoid getting overwhelmed by the complexity of physiology, we needed only to break it down into its component parts. I'll follow her example here, and I promise to keep it simple and short.

When an individual undergoes repeated endurance exercise bouts, body systems adapt to that exercise and make the body more efficient. All bodily functions require energy, and the beauty of the human system is that bodily functions adapt to the exercise to be more efficient in delivering the needed energy.

The heart. We all know that the heart is a muscle. We also know that when we train a muscle, it becomes more fit. The heart is no different. During regular, sustained exercise, the heart muscle walls adapt by becoming thicker and stronger. This strengthening in turn permits a stronger and more efficient push of the blood, compared to an untrained heart, and the stronger push is welcomed by the other parts of the body, which need the blood's nutrients and oxygen.

The increase in the heart's size and efficiency is evident when a physician or nurse takes the pulse of a trained individual. An untrained individual may have a normal resting heart rate of, say, 65 beats per minute, but a trained athlete can easily have a resting heartbeat in the 40s. Training the heart brings about other changes, too, most notably in size. In fact, the trained heart can be so significantly larger that it is sometimes called an "athlete's heart," and its appearance on an X-ray or echocardiogram is easily distinguished by trained eyes from an abnormal enlargement.

The lungs and respiration. We all see when we exercise that we breathe faster. Our breathing rate goes up because we need more oxygen to help our internal energy factories burn fuel, and breathing faster helps us get that oxygen flowing. That's quite obvious, but how does that square with what we see at the finish line of a race, where marathon winners walk around easily, not at all out of breath and looking like they just strolled around the block? The reason for the lack of drama is simple: The lungs also become more efficient with training and adapt to take in more air with each breath. The increased lung capacity is normal, and you will benefit from this expected result of training as well. You'll breathe easier; you will be able to handle greater distances, more hills, and more frequent exercise; and your body will respond with greater vigor and better overall health.

Muscle cells. The strength demands you place on your body during regular exercise require your muscle cells to become more efficient in their use of the nutrients brought to them by the blood. Muscle cells adapt to training by increasing the mitochondria components of their cells. Mitochondria are the "power source" of the cell in that they are a structure where these nutrients are made into energy (food and oxygen go in, and energy comes out). More mitochondria lead to more oxygen-processing capacity and thus to greater energy, so the muscle cells concentrate on increasing mitochondrial density in response to exercise.

Redirection of blood flow. When you run (or walk or bike) a significant distance (at least 5 kilometers, or about 3 miles), the blood vessels in the legs dilate (become larger) to enhance blood flow to and from the leg muscles. Similarly, more blood flow also goes to the skin to enhance cooling.

After exercise stops, these vessels temporarily maintain their open (dilated) state. At the same time, the "pumping action" of muscles, which helps return blood to the heart, also stops. And that's why you see those marathon racers continuing to walk steadily once they've crossed the finish line; they're working to keep the blood flowing until normal blood circulation resumes. So remember when you finish a long run to allow at least 10 minutes for a cooldown walk. Add it to your routine, and you'll avoid the possibility of a blackout ("syncope") due to too much blood in your legs and not enough elsewhere (see the sidebar on syncope later in this section).

Training 101: What to Do During Training to Help Achieve Success at Your Event

Training prepares your muscles, ligaments, tendons, heart, lungs, and entire body for your event. It is also YOUR time to practice. You should practice not only how you will maneuver over hills (interval training), but also how you will eat, drink, and react to pain or injury on race day. The first (and most important) rule of endurance medicine is "Don't do anything new on race day!" Practice these strategies now, in training, so that you will be ready for your race.

Please remember that you are an experiment unto yourself. The greatest mistake made by participants is relying on the advice of others rather than experimenting for themselves. You should practice, experiment, and have fun figuring out what works best for your body. My basic recommendations are as follows:

Drink water. For athletes, water is the drink of choice for both general health and endurance training lasting less than 30 minutes.

Use sports drinks on longer runs. Sports drinks are recommended exclusively for runs/walks/biking lasting more than 30 minutes. Train to use these drinks undiluted; do not mix them with water. The added carbohydrates and electrolytes speed absorption of fluids and add calories for energy. There is actually decreased benefit to watering down or diluting sports drinks or alternating sports drinks with water because doing so decreases your performance and your body's ability to handle the stress of an endurance event.

Train with your sports drink before you race with it. As you begin training for your chosen event, find out which sports drink will be available along the course. I always suggest trying this drink during training. You will find that there are some drinks that your body simply does not like during training (you'll feel bloated or feel that you are not digesting them well). If you don't like the drink that will be available, make preparations to use an alternate sports drink on event day (that is, carry your own in a "Fuel Belt" around your waist, or something similar).

Drink when you're thirsty. Rely on your thirst mechanism to indicate signs of dehydration. New research shows this to be the best indicator! You're unique, so don't copy what other participants do. Some people need less fluid than you, whereas others need more. Learn your individual hydration needs by focusing on your thirst mechanism: When you're thirsty, have something to drink.

Maintain a healthy level of hydration. It is vital to stay well hydrated throughout the day. The color of your urine should be similar to the yellow color of lemonade. Urine that is darker (like iced tea) or approaches an amber color is a signal that you are dehydrated and need to drink fluids. Urine that is clear like water means you are overhydrated.

Eat balanced meals. As an athlete (competitive or recreational), your body must be fueled optimally to exercise effectively. To maintain or improve strength, speed, and stamina, consume adequate amounts of carbohydrates, protein, and fat. Most studies agree that a daily diet of 55–65 percent carbohydrates, 15–20 percent protein, and 20–30 percent fat is ideal. Although this concept is great in theory, most people have a difficult time accurately applying it to their everyday lives. The U.S. Department of Agriculture came up with the Food Guide Pyramid to help put these healthy guidelines into practice. Do not get too compulsive about this; do your best to approximate your food intake based on the pyramid. Should you need personal, more specific advice, ask your physician to recommend a registered dietitian/nutritionist in your area.

Eating meals high *only* in carbohydrates for lunch and dinner pretraining or pre-race is *not* recommended. Do your best to follow the food guidelines just outlined at all times. It is very important to experiment (during training) to find the "right" foods for your body.

Avoid heavy fats. Emphasize healthy foods in your diet while limiting fried and high-fat foods.

Always eat breakfast. Practice your pretraining or pre-race breakfast, and experiment in regard to food selection. A bagel with jelly, a glass of orange juice, and a banana make a terrific breakfast and create a solid base for exercise. If you want a one-plate meal, I especially recommend what I call the "Elvis bagel": a bagel of your choice with peanut butter and banana. It covers all the bases, with the bagel for carbohydrate, the peanut butter for an excellent source of protein, and the banana for immediate energy.

No matter what you choose, the most important advice I can give here is to make sure that you eat something before heading out, and leave a little time to digest it. No fuel means poor performance. Balanced fuel means you'll run longer and better. If you're not heading out right after breakfast, then eat a light snack in the morning prior to your training session.

Do "the salt." For triathlon training or run/walk events of 10K or longer, it is important to maintain your salt level and hydration. For that reason, I ask all participants to practice "the salt" (as long as your doctor has not restricted your salt intake). Prior to event day, get two small packets of salt (found at all fast-food restaurants). Just before you start, pour one packet of salt on your hand and lick it; the salt will be absorbed in your mouth. Halfway through the event (or training session), lick the second packet of salt. Maintaining your salt level and hydration will help you feel great at the end of your training session or event. It is not wise to use salt tablets or capsules because with the decreased blood flow to the stomach resulting from the blood being diverted to your legs, this form of salt will be irritative to the stomach lining and not well absorbed.

Use energy gels in moderation. Consider trying the "gel" carbohydrate replacement products. Be sure to chase them down with water (approximately 6 to 8 ounces) to avoid stomach cramps and ensure absorption. These gels should be used sparingly during exercise; once or twice is more than enough if you eat and drink properly beforehand. Consuming too much gel will cause the release of insulin, creating a yo-yo effect of sugar highs and lows that will have a negative impact on the way you feel. Again, practice, practice, practice before the event so that you can see how your body reacts and responds!

Always actively cool down after a run. After completing your training, walk for a few minutes at an easy pace, as this continued movement helps to ensure your blood flow goes from your legs back to the rest of your body. How long should you walk? No specific

The Maalox Marathoner

When I take part in expert panels at the Rock 'n' Roll Marathons, the questions usually come from the audience. But one time, Frank Shorter, gold medalist at the 1972 Olympics, had the best question of the day. He said, "I used to take some antacid before I ran and it made me feel better when I finished. Any reason for this?"

In fact, there is a very good reason. As you know from reading "Endurance Physiology 101" in this chapter, when anyone runs a significant distance, blood is naturally directed to the legs. (Even if you didn't know this, you would soon learn it if you tried to feed a runner immediately after a race. What happens? It comes right back up! They vomit because blood has been directed away from the stomach and normal peristaltic movement has ceased or slowed to a crawl. This is why the first rule of running medicine is always to stand to the side of a runner, never directly in front!)

Frank used to feel nauseous at the end of runs because, with blood flow directed away from the stomach, the stomach lining was deprived of normal blood flow and could not handle the acid load. Taking an antacid like Rolaids, Tums, Mylanta, or Maalox in a tablet or one teaspoon prior to the run helps buffer that acid and makes you feel better at the end.

Thanks to Frank, now everyone can benefit from this tip.

guideline has ever been published, but we know that the more you walk, the better your body will redirect the blood from your legs to the rest of your body, and the better you'll feel the next day. After a marathon, 10 minutes of walking would not be too much, and 15 minutes would be better.

Eat and drink after you cool down. After walking, have something to eat and drink. Sports drinks are recommended for the electrolytes and sugar they contain to replace depleted glycogen (muscle fuel) stores (electrolytes are the free ions on that help regulate the hydration in your body, maintain proper blood pH, and contribute to nerve and muscle function). Research has shown that to avoid muscle fatigue the next day, athletes should eat carbohydrates as soon as possible following long-duration exercise.

Try recovery drinks for muscle repair. A "recovery drink" that has carbs and added protein in it is best (3:1 to 4:1 carbohydrate to protein) for giving you the amino acids necessary for muscle repair. If you do not have a recovery drink, be sure to eat protein in your next meal. Peanut butter and jelly sandwiches and chocolate milk are good food alternatives to the commercial sports drinks.

Don't delay early treatment of aches or injuries. If you develop a pain during training that causes you to change your form, see a sports medicine physician immediately. Usually, early diagnosis and treatment will ensure little or no time away from your training. If you decide to wait, you could be out for much longer or be forced to defer your event altogether. Again, because no two people are exactly alike, get proper help early.

Training for Success: The Week Before the Event

As you scale back on the distance and intensity of your training during that last week before the race, realize that your body will not be burning as many calories. If you don't reduce the quantity of your food servings early in the week, you may gain one or two pounds. My recommended guidelines for the week before your race are as follows:

Choose high-quality, nutrient-dense foods. Use care in selecting foods to eat during this time period. Aim for eating quality foods rather than snacking on high-fat products. Desirable foods that are high in carbohydrate, moderate in protein, and low in fat include rice, cereal, pasta, oatmeal, eggs, and potatoes, and sandwiches with roast beef, turkey, ham, or peanut butter and jelly. High-fat foods you should avoid include bacon, steak, sausage, ice cream, and foods with thick or creamy sauces. Salads are fine, but even with additions of fish or chicken, they tend to be low in carbohydrates and low in calories.

Stock your body's hydration needs in advance. Hydrate well the week before your event (water is best). Research has shown that carbohydrates convert to glycogen (the storage form of carbohydrate you will need during the race) more effectively when accompanied by the consumption of water. This is the time when you probably will

Plan and Practice What You're Going to Eat and Drink

Not long ago, I was helping a runner at a finish-line medical tent. After he was done ruining my shoes by depositing his dinner from the night before on them, he whimpered, "Doc, I don't understand it. I did everything right. I even pasta-loaded last night." I responded, "Then maybe spaghetti and meatballs weren't 'the right thing,' do you think?"

Understanding what to eat during training, the days leading up to the marathon, the night before, during the event, and after it is not simple and requires some thought and preparation. Your food is your fuel, and your body reacts to different food groups in different ways. Carbo-loading—the forced storing of that precious muscle fuel, glycogen—has become a science. There are now energy gels, like the world-famous product GU, placed strategically along the courses of many marathons and half-marathons.

The smart marathoner plans in advance what to eat for maximal performance. Eat smart and you'll not only feel good; you also won't need new shoes!

gain a couple of pounds, but don't worry about it. This will be the fuel you will use during your race!

Dial back on alcohol. In the week before your event, cut your alcohol consumption to a minimum, or eliminate it altogether. Alcohol dehydrates the body, which is exactly what you don't want before a race.

Pack healthy foods for travel. If you are traveling out of town, be sure to pack healthy snack foods you may wish to eat during event weekend. Doing so will eliminate the need to search for a grocery store that stocks your favorite foods.

Drink water on the plane. If traveling by plane to your event destination, carry bottled water with you (remember you will need to purchase this in the airport once you have cleared security). Flying at high altitudes causes dehydration.

Stick to your proven training diet. Be sure to eat all food products that have been "tried and proven" during your training period. Keep pasta sauces simple, avoiding high-fat varieties (Alfredo, pesto, and similar toppings). Now is *not* the moment to try Mexican food for the first time!

Avoid eating differently the night before the event. This is *not* your last meal, and if you eat differently than usual, you may feel sick on race day.

Unless you eat lots of greens regularly, avoid eating a big salad or vegetables (roughage) the night before your race as these may cause digestive problems on race day. If you are used to them, you can probably get away with eating some, but don't overdo it. Stick to water during the evening meal. Because coffee and tea contain caffeine, these products may make it difficult for you to fall asleep easily.

Stay away from anti-inflammatories. Stop taking nonsteroidal anti-inflammatory drugs (such as Advil, Motrin, Aleve, ibuprofen, and naproxen), as these have proven to be a risk factor for hyponatremia (low sodium level and high cellular water level), a serious condition you want to avoid (see the sidebar on syncope and hyponatremia on page 28). You should also avoid a full dose (325 mg) of aspirin. However, if you are taking a baby aspirin once a day for your heart, that low dose does not have a significant nonsteroidal effect and can be safely continued. Acetaminophen (Tylenol) is safe during this period and during your event. You may restart an NSAID six hours after you finish the event.

Watch your meds. Do not take dehydrating cold medicines, anti-allergy meds, or antidiarrhea medications before or during the event.

Racing for Success: Your Race Day Plan

The best way to have a good race is to stick to your training plan. Don't do anything new! Instead, approach your race or event in the same way that you handled each training run. Of course, you may be nervous and excited, and that adrenaline may carry you to the finish line in record time. But don't let your emotions get the best of you, and don't let any doubts about your readiness lead you into rash, last-minute decisions. If you've trained and prepared well, then you've done everything right to get ready for this special day. Enjoy yourself, and keep the following guidelines in mind.

Race as you trained. On race day morning, eat and drink as you did during your training. Don't forget your Elvis bagel! (See page 22.)

Take a baby aspirin. As long as your doctor approves, take one baby aspirin (81 mg) on race morning to help avoid cardiac problems.

Limit caffeine. Keep your caffeine intake below 200 mg; that's about 2 cups of coffee.

Hit the port-o-potty. When you get to the race venue, immediately get in line for the port-o-potty! This may sound funny, but clearing your waste prior to the start makes good sense. The excitement and anticipation of the event will make you want to clear that waste at some point; doing it before you start may help you avoid looking for a place along the route.

Avoiding Syncope and Hyponatremia

"Syncope" is the medical term for a blackout, and for runners the most common experience of syncope is just after finishing a long training run or a race. As we discussed earlier in "Endurance Physiology 101" (see page 19), when you run a significant distance (at least 5 kilometers, or about 3 miles), blood is redirected to your legs to supply the muscles with oxygen and away from your internal organs, including your stomach and kidneys. The blood vessels in the legs open up, or dilate, to carry more oxygen-rich blood, and the leg muscles respond to that blood flow with greater energy capacity.

This is all well and good, but we have to remember that after exercise stops, these vessels temporarily maintain their dilated state. With more blood volume but no pumping action to move that blood, it pools in the lower extremities. And if an athlete is standing, rather than walking, after exercising, the blood collecting in the legs means less blood available to the brain, and syncope can result. Some athletes will experience warning signs, such as lightheadedness, nausea, and visual disturbance, prior to syncope. This is not a serious condition, and it is entirely normal. It can be prevented by walking after you finish.

The initial treatment for an athlete who has blacked out is to lay him or her down and elevate the legs (for more detail, see "Exercise-Associated Collapse" in Part II). We then ice down (or use cool water on) the legs and massage the legs upward toward the heart. The athlete will usually come around in a few seconds. Once awake and alert, the athlete will be helped to a sitting position, in stages, slowly over the next 15 to 20 minutes: First the legs are lowered to the body level, then the athlete is encouraged to sit up, then the legs are dangled off the cot, and finally the athlete is helped up and helped to walk. We encourage the athlete to drink fluids only after up and

Do "the salt." Lick one fast-food packet of salt right before you start (as you did in training; see page 23), and carry a second packet for consumption halfway through.

Obey your body's signs of thirst. At fluid stations along the race route, drink no more than 1 cup (8 ounces) of fluid every 20 minutes while walking/running. Drink based on your thirst level. Although it's okay to drink plain water in the early miles, you should consume sports beverages after 30 minutes of continuous exertion. During your training, you found out what works best for you. Stick to that plan unless race conditions are vastly different from your training

walking; blood flow has to return to the stomach so that the fluids travel in the proper direction! The few athletes who don't respond to this conservative treatment likely have a more serious underlying medical condition and will have a more in-depth evaluation at a hospital.

While blood flow is being redirected to the legs, it is also moving away from the kidneys, which regulate salt; normally, if the salt level in the blood is too low, the kidneys conserve salt, and if it is too high, they remove it. However, the physiology of the kidneys changes when blood flow decreases; they become what are often termed "endurance kidneys" or "marathon kidneys," which unfortunately urinate out too much salt and retain too much water in the body. This may lead to a condition called hyponatremia (too little salt in blood serum), which can be dangerous. Your blood pressure drops, and you can become dizzy. You may get a headache, become confused, or suffer hallucinations. You may also develop muscle spasms or cramps or become sick to your stomach. Drinking too much water or sports drink can lead to this condition, which mimics exercise-associated collapse (EAC). Therefore, it's important to follow the drinking guidelines successfully used in training during both training and events, use salt as described, and seek medical attention at a medical tent if you don't feel well.

Also keep in mind that nonsteroidal anti-inflammatory drugs (NSAIDs), such as Advil, Motrin, Aleve, ibuprofen, aspirin, and naproxen, can increase the possibility of hyponatremia by decreasing blood flow to the kidneys further and interfering with a hormone that helps the body retain salt (a dose a day of baby aspirin is okay). Stop taking NSAIDs 24 hours before your endurance training or race, and do not start again until at least 6 hours have passed following the completion of your training/event, you are able to drink fluids without nausea or vomiting, you have urinated once, and you feel physically and mentally back to normal. Acetaminophen (Tylenol) has proven to be safe. Do not use anything but acetaminophen, if needed.

mileage. Gauge the distance between fluid stations, and decide beforehand whether or not you should bring and carry your own sports drink. Every race is different. Be prepared.

Water is usually offered at the first tables at a fluid station, with sports beverages usually served near the end of the station. If you choose to drink while moving through the stations, squeeze the top of the cup into a "V" shape to create a smooth delivery of fluid directly into your mouth. If you decide instead to stop and drink, please get out of the way of other participants. Drink only what quenches your thirst; do not overdrink!

Use gels only if you are used to them. If you've used gels during your training, continue to use them as part of your normal routine. Do not consume more than usual on race day. Again, do not try anything new!

Finish "the salt." Halfway through the event, lick the second fast-food packet of salt (as you did in training).

Don't be afraid to seek aid. If you feel sick or are having pain that causes you to change your running/walking style, stop at a medical aid station. At these stations, volunteer physicians and medical personnel are there to help you. Take advantage of these free services to ensure a healthy and successful finish.

After the Event

After the event, make sure to do the following:

Walk to cool down. After crossing the finish line, walk, walk, and walk some more. It is important that your blood flow goes back from your legs to the rest of your body. The blood that has been naturally directed to your legs during the event now needs to get back to your stomach before you eat and drink.

Drink after you have cooled down. After walking for about 10–15 minutes, get something to drink (water, sports drink). Although it may be tempting, hold off on consuming alcoholic beverages until later in the evening if you feel so inclined (if you are over the age of 21).

Eat after drinking. After you can keep fluid down normally, grab something to eat. Try bananas, tomato juice, peanut butter and jelly sandwiches, orange juice, chocolate milk, or the scientific recovery drink you practiced with during training.

Take care of any medical concerns. If you have any medical concerns or questions, go to a medical aid station and inquire before leaving the venue. There are volunteer physicians and medical personnel available to help you. Take advantage of this free service.

Steer clear of the massage table for at least two hours. *Do not* have a postevent massage within the first two hours of finishing the race. Research has shown that the lactic acid built up in muscles needs that time to "buffer" back to a neutral pH so as not to cause further damage and postevent soreness. Having a light massage between two and eight hours after event completion has proven to be beneficial in preventing postevent soreness, so book an appointment with a local therapist during that window of time. Do not have deep tissue work for at least three to five days after an endurance event, for the same reasons.

No new stretches. Your post-race muscles are friable. If you put them through a stretch they're not used to, you can easily injure them.

Training Smart: How to Work Together with Your Doctor and Coach

The question I most frequently refuse to answer when my patients ask it is, "How should I train?" I'm a sports physician. I do doctoring. Training is for coaches. Just as I don't want coaches making diagnoses, I know they don't want me making training decisions for their runners.

But when my patients are injured or have some other medical problem, I can help them get back as quickly as possible to whatever speed and workout schedule they had achieved so far with their coaches. Whether a series of fast-tempo intervals will make you a speedier runner is up to your coach. Whether your balky Achilles tendon will tolerate those speed sessions at all is up to me. That's how we'll work together.

I have found, by the way, that endurance participants gearing up for a race definitely do their best under the tutelage of a good coach. So find a good one. Then you will be in a position to make the play yourself and turn your next marathon adventure into a complete success.

Avoid a hot shower right after the race. At home (or at the hotel) avoid taking a hot shower. A hot shower will only increase inflammation of stressed muscles and joints. Most sports physicians recommend a cool shower or iced bath (add ice cubes to your bath) or an ice massage to cool down muscles and reduce inflammation.

Eat a balanced meal. After you return home (or to the hotel), have a nice lunch. This should be a well-balanced meal in which the majority of the total calories are carbohydrates. However, don't forget to consume at least 20 percent of the total calories from protein sources in order to give you the amino acids that you need to repair your muscles.

Restart NSAIDs after six hours. Six hours after you have finished, and once you are able to drink without nausea or vomiting, have urinated once, and feel physically and mentally back to normal, you can use your favorite headache, anti-inflammatory, or pain reliever that your doctor has recommended.

Congratulations! And now it's time to think about your next event.

Getting the Best Equipment

Just because you have only one principal piece of equipment to purchase doesn't mean you can't go wrong. Too many running shoe stores seem to hire perfectly cordial people who have a way of sounding like experts but who in fact have little to no real training in fitting running shoes. If you're in one of those stores, chances are good that within the blink of an eye the salesperson will have you in a shoe that seems perfect for you when, in reality, it's a shoe that the store has too many of and that the salesperson has been instructed to move. Know this: Rarely does a shoe store actually train its salespeople adequately in what kinds of individuals should be in which kinds of shoes! They have not gone to a health professional school, and their knowledge is very limited at best.

Be aware that this book can't help you with specific, model-by-model recommendations either. Shoes change often, new models come out each season, and even experienced runners who replace their shoes regularly complain that as soon as they've settled on a model as a good, long-term choice, it goes right out of production. But I'll give you easy-to-follow guidelines to help you find the proper shoes. Armed with my guidelines, you will not be fooled or steered in the wrong direction. You will be ready to make that proper purchase.

Finding the Right Running Shoes

Looking at the walls of running shoes in sporting goods stores can be intimidating, but there are some easy ways to narrow your choices. First, you pretty much get what you pay for when it comes to features and quality, so prepare to spend in the $90 to $140 range for good shoes. You'll need to get adequate cushioning, good forefoot flexibility, enough toe box room (assuming the shoe is fitted correctly), and a strong heel counter to support your weight.

Just don't make your choice in the morning. Always try on shoes at the end of the day when your feet are swollen, and see that there's at least one thumbnail length of distance between the end of your longest toe and the end of the shoe. If you're an overpronator—that is, if your

Figure I.1

The parts of the running shoe

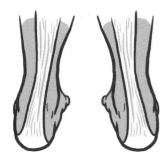

Figure I.2A
Pronator

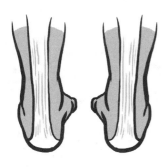

Figure I.2B
Neutral

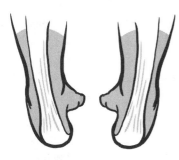

Figure I.2C
Supinator

foot rolls inward more than your body can deal with without pain—you may also need to be fitted for a custom orthotic to go into the shoe to protect you from injury (see page 68 for more on orthotics). Even top footwear can only do so much.

When it comes to slapping feet on the ground, most everyone falls into one of three gait categories. **Pronators** roll their feet inward. They may have flat feet with no arches or small arches, but they can also have feet with high arches and wide forefoots (the so-called Irish foot; see "The Myth of Arches" sidebar for more information). These types of feet are good candidates for motion control shoes. **Neutral** runners keep their feet square to the ground and should look for stability shoes. **Supinators** (or underpronators) have outwardly rolling feet and usually have high arches and will generally benefit from cushioned shoes.

If you're not sure which group you belong to, you can ask your coach or sports doctor. They can look at the wear pattern on your old shoes to help identify your gait and pick new shoes that will work best for your running style.

Before you purchase a shoe, inspect it for defects in workmanship (poor stitching, misaligned upper to lower shoe, or heel counters that roll in or out). If you are buying multiple pairs at the same time, I highly recommend that you buy the same make and model. That is, as long as you are training comfortably, you should not buy different models and switch off during the week. Now obviously if you start to have problems, your doctor may say that you need to change shoes. Otherwise, stick to one brand and one style to avoid making your feet adapt to different shoes on different days.

When you've got your shoes, you're ready to go. The new ones need virtually no breaking in for regular training. However, you should not buy new shoes right before a race or other big event; you need to wear them for a couple of weeks before they and your feet become familiar enough with each other to avoid problems. Note, too, that if you develop a pain with your new shoes that changes your form, give your doc a call before you do more damage.

New running shoes should be purchased every six months, regardless of wear, or every 500 miles, whichever comes first.

Understanding Shoe Groups

I separate shoes into four groups. If you take this guide to the shoe store and ask for the shoe in the group you fit into, you will be at a good place to start your running.

GROUP 1 SHOES
MOTION CONTROL SHOES

These are good for most runners but are required for the following:

- Severe overpronators: runners with low-arched or inwardly rolling feet
- Heavy runners: runners weighing 180 pounds or more
- High-mileage runners: runners who run more than 30 miles/week
- Often injured runners: runners who lost more than four weeks of training in the last year due to running injuries
- Walkers: any walker

GROUP 2 SHOES
STABILITY SHOES

These are good for most runners but are best for the following:

- Mild to moderate pronators: runners whose shoes do not break down on the inner side
- Midweight or female runners: runners weighing less than 180 pounds
- Moderate-mileage runners: runners who run about 15 to 30 miles/week
- Orthotic wearers: runners who run in orthotics or arch supports
- Seldom-injured runners: runners who missed less than four weeks in the last year

The Myth of Arches

For as long as I can remember, conventional wisdom has said that you can tell what kind of shoes you need by looking at your footprint. If you have flat feet, you're a pronator and need a motion control shoe. If you have a normal arch, you should get a stability shoe. If you have a high arch, you're a supinator and need a cushioned shoe.

This advice has been repeated in countless magazine stories and running books, usually accompanied by illustrations showing you how to step on a piece of wet tissue paper to divine the

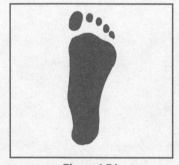

Figure I.3A

Low arch

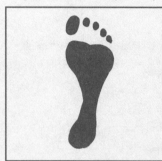

Figure I.3B

Normal arch

Figure I.3C

High arch

height of your arch, as if you were reading tea leaves. And shoe salespeople in the mass market stores have trays of sand and reams of marketing information to reinforce this notion.

The only problem: It's not true.

When I see patients about their shoes, I have them run barefoot on a treadmill. Within a few strides, I can see their gait and easily determine what kind of shoe they need. I can also see whether they may need a corrective orthotic. I often check their arches, too, and what I have found is that while there is some correlation between arch type and gait, the situation isn't anywhere near as cut-and-dried as the "experts" would have you believe.

The best example of this is when I see patients and ask them if they have Irish blood in them. They look at me with a shocked expression: How would I know that? The "Irish foot" is a thin heel, high arch, wide forefoot. If you looked at a wet imprint, you'd call this a supinator. But when running, these folks are obvious overpronators, coming down on the outside of the foot with an exaggerated roll to the inside.

The real key to choosing a shoe is to know your gait: pronator, neutral, supinator. If you aren't sure where you fit in, see a qualified sports medicine professional with specific experience in running gait and form. Because while your arches offer some interesting information about the conformation of your feet, they don't necessarily tell the whole story about the way you run.

GROUP 3 SHOES

CUSHIONED SHOES

These are a poor choice for most runners except the following:

- Supinators (underpronators): runners with high-arched or outwardly rolling feet
- Beginners: runners who run less than 15 miles/week
- Lightweights: runners who are seldom injured and weigh less than 140 pounds

GROUP 4 SHOES

LIGHTWEIGHT TRAINERS

These are never good for daily training! These shoes are too unstable and light to provide the proper stability and cushion needed for daily training. They can and should be used for competition or time trial racing.

Cold Weather Running Tips

If race day is unusually cold or damp, please follow these guidelines to stay safe:

Stay warm before the race. If race morning is cold and/or wet, take care not to arrive far in advance of the race start. This way you'll avoid standing too long in the cold. Wearing extra clothing, such as long pants, a long-sleeved shirt, and a wind-resistant jacket, will keep your body warm and make you less prone to injury. Wearing layered clothes that you don't care about and can throw away along the route is sometimes a good idea. Spend a little extra time jogging in place to warm your muscles before starting.

Respect your limits. Cold temperatures restrict blood flow, which can cause muscles to contract and even cramp. You will feel stiff and tight, especially in the early miles, if you don't warm up. If you try to force the pace, you may pull (tear) a muscle. Adjust your pace to allow your body a little extra time to warm up. You may have to slow down from your projected pace to get to the finish line safely.

Protect yourself from the elements. Prepare yourself by wearing a hat and gloves, and even a face mask or scarf to cover your neck and face. Remember that wind increases the effects of the cold; you may risk frostbite on unprotected areas on a cold, windy day. Apply a sweat-resistant sport moisturizer for extra protection, and apply lip balm. Also apply petroleum jelly for any spots prone to chafing or chapping. (Never assume the medical team will have these for you: Be prepared like a good Boy or Girl Scout!)

Wear synthetic fabrics, and layer your clothing. Cold temperatures necessitate long pants, long sleeves, and extra layers of clothing. Keep the fabric closest to your body synthetic, preferably of sweat-wicking material, and make sure it fits snugly. Your top layer should be wind-resistant and waterproof if there's rain or snow. You can also purchase arm sleeves that can be adjusted, or removed, once you've warmed up. If possible, test all clothing in advance to make sure it's warm and comfortable to race in. And be sure to change out of your wet clothes as soon as possible after you finish.

Know the signs of hypothermia and frostbite. *Hypothermia* occurs when your body temperature falls below 95 degrees; symptoms can include confusion and uncontrollable shivering. *Frostbite* occurs when circulation is restricted in the extremities (fingers, toes, ears, and nose); symptoms can include feeling numb and turning white or blue. Pay attention to your body during the race, and watch for these symptoms. Please seek medical attention at a medical aid station if you are not sure or are feeling bad.

Don't forget to drink: not too much and not too little. In cold weather it is easy to overlook your fluid needs, but it is not safe to ignore them. The best rule of thumb during exercise is to drink for thirst and no more than 1 cup (8 ounces) of fluid every 20 minutes. Your body is still sweating underneath those layers of clothing, so replenish your fluids appropriately.

Shorten your stride in snow, ice, sleet, or heavy rain. If there is snow, ice, or excessive water on the ground, shorten your stride and pay attention to your footing and the runners around you to avoid a slip or fall. Black ice is a real danger for slippage and consequent sprains and broken bones. Do not expect to attain a personal record (PR) in these conditions; instead, plan for a safe race.

Warm Weather Racing Tips

Races in the heat require planning and forethought. You cannot race well when you are unprepared for the heat or when you travel from someplace cold to someplace warm. It takes your body a good 7 to 10 days to acclimatize.

To stay healthy in hot weather, I recommend the following:

Run within your capability. Do not push yourself in the heat. The greatest cause of heat illness is running too hard in hot conditions.

Eat a good pre-race meal a few hours before the run. Try an "Elvis bagel" (peanut butter and banana) during your training: It has protein and carbs.

Limit caffeine. Keep your total intake (including gels) to 200 mg; that's about 2 cups of coffee.

Do "the salt"! Eat salted foods all week prior to the event. On race day, consume one fast-food salt packet at the start line. Have another salt packet halfway through the race.

Start the race well hydrated. Check your urine. If it is light yellow, like lemonade, you are drinking perfectly. If it is clear, you are drinking too much. If your urine looks like iced tea, you are not drinking enough!

Do not overdrink. Drinking too much is as bad as not drinking enough. The best way to drink healthy is to drink only when you're thirsty. Nevertheless, drink no more than 1 cup (8 ounces) every 20 minutes while running or walking.

Choose sports drinks over water. Practice in training to do this. If you are exercising 30 minutes or more, research shows that sports drinks from the bottle are the healthiest way to go (do not dilute them or alternate them with water or a combo of a gel and water). Sports drinks are expertly prepared with energy (sugar) and salt.

Use the spray stations along the course, if provided, and at the finish to cool off. If you are overheating, a water spray will cool you down quickly and have a lasting effect as the water evaporates from your skin. Keep in mind, however, that drenched clothing will cling to skin and prevent evaporation, and wet socks can cause blisters, so use this strategy wisely. If there are no spray stations, dump a cup of water—not sticky sports drink!—over your head.

Protect yourself from the sun. Wear a cap or visor to shield your head, face, and eyes from the sun's burning rays, and wear sunglasses to protect your eyes. Use sunscreen on exposed skin, even on overcast days.

Check your meds. Do not consume cold medicines that contain ephedrine or pseudoephedrine, or antidiarrhea medicines with dehydrating agents in them. They may increase your risk for heat illness. Caffeine products are OK only in doses you are used to during training (and in any case less than 200 mg, or 2 cups of coffee). Do not start taking a caffeine product on race day if you have not used one before.

Wear synthetic fabrics. Unlike cotton, synthetics wick moisture from your skin so that cooling evaporation can occur. Synthetics also decrease chafing and don't cling and cause a chill. Look for loose-fitting garments with mesh inserts under the arms, on the sides of the torso, down the arms, and on the outer thighs. Acrylic socks keep feet dry and cool.

Seek help if you need it. If you feel overly warm or just "not right," stop at a medical station along the course or at the finish and get checked out by a physician.

Finish steady. Do not sprint the last mile. Instead, run the final stretch as you did in your training.

Find some ice. Apply iced towels or ice bags behind your neck at the finish to help you feel cooler faster.

If you follow all these recommendations, you will feel great and enjoy the summer running season.

Traveling to a Desert Race

Before the first PF Chang's Rock 'n' Roll Marathon in Arizona, I would have told you to do "nothing new" to prepare for the race weekend as the only worry would be dehydration. And not one case in the history of the world has been reported of someone dying of dehydration from running a race.

This all changed with what I learned in Arizona. When I went to all the potential receiving hospitals' emergency rooms (ERs) to give my standard inservice about hyponatremia to ER personnel, all the docs told me that in the desert's dry climate we would see dehydration at a significant level. They were right. Since then, the Las Vegas Rock 'n' Roll Marathon has reported similar results.

Therefore, when you are traveling from a nondry climate to a dry one, please follow these recommendations so that you do not start the race dehydrated:

Get there early. Try to arrive at the dry climate at least three to four days before the event. It takes a good three days to acclimate.

Drink water on the plane. If traveling by air, drink water or sports drink during the flight. The airlines serve drinks to passengers because they know that altitude is dehydrating. The longer your flight is, the more dehydrated you can become unless you offset the effects by drinking regularly.

Monitor your fluid intake. During the flight and on race day before and during the event, check your urine for hydration status. Remember: You want lemonade color. Clear urine means that you are drinking too much; iced-tea color, that you are drinking too little.

Do "the salt." This is very important in the desert. Add salt to your diet as well for the three days before the event. Of course, do this only with your doctor's permission. See page 23 for a complete explanation on how to use salt packets.

Drink for thirst. But if you aren't yet great at this, try to remember: 1 cup (8 ounces) every 20 to 30 minutes.

Avoid anti-inflammatories. Do not use NSAIDs from 24 hours before the race until you finish and are eating and drinking normally and have lemonade-color urine. NSAIDs increase your risk for hyponatremia, and you don't want an extra burden on your body.

If you do all these, the only thing you will notice about desert races is how much fun you are actually having.

PART II
MARATHONS AND HALF-MARATHONS

Marathons and Half-Marathons

A Race for Everyone

These days, you hear that marathons and half-marathons are for everybody. How did that happen? Who turned the notoriously grueling 26.2-mile marathon (or 13.1-mile half-marathon) footrace into something that now looks like fun (at least from the sidelines)?

As I stand with the medical support teams at roadside aid stations and in finish-line tents during marathons, half-marathons, and 5K and 10K races across the country, I see beaming men and women, from teens to octogenarians, running and walking the distance. These healthy people of all ages and descriptions exemplify what exercising is all about today. Young and old, thin and not so thin, from all racial and ethnic backgrounds, they have replaced what was once the typically gaunt, sweaty, exhausted male runner, grimly intense, glaring at his watch in the hope that he can shave a few seconds off his PR.

Today the sport's appeal has broadened. In many ways, participating is an adventure. For most, the goal is not to attack the course or conquer the distance, but rather to enjoy the event as a personal challenge. The long-distance test of endurance has a whole new look. Instead of race day being a final exam after all the training, it has become a training celebration, an experience to be savored.

Increasingly, we know that almost anyone can run or walk a 5K (3.1 miles), 10K (6.2 miles), half-marathon (13.1 miles), or marathon (26.2 miles). In fact, approximately 2 million Americans are now crossing the finish line of a road race each year, having either run or walked, and the numbers continue to grow. I think it's wonderful and amazing that 44 million Americans say they run as a sport and that 10.7 million say they run a minimum of 100 days throughout the year. Of these, 55 percent are men and 45 percent are women. But the gender gap is shrinking, and some races actually have more women than men!

The even more gratifying news is that so many people are running and walking these long-distance events for recreation and fundraising. Bands are playing, cheerleaders are holding competitions along the course, spectators are lining the streets cheering the participants and holding their own parties, and hundreds of millions of dollars are being raised for countless worthy causes. The race weekend is a major financial boon to a community, as hotels fill and restaurant reservations become impossible to get on race weekend.

Participation in road races is going through the roof. Statistics compiled by the USA Track & Field Road Running Information Center show that whereas in 1980 there were only 120,000 marathon finishers (90 percent, or 108,000, of them male and only 10 percent, or 12,000, of them female), by 1991 there were 274,000 finishers (221,940 male, or 81 percent, and 52,060 female, or 19 percent)—in other words, a fourfold increase in women participants in 11 years. In 1999, we saw 435,000 marathon finishers, 282,750 male (65 percent) and 152,250 female (35 percent). That's a fourfold increase in the total number of participants and a *twelvefold* increase in the total number of female participants! There are now more women finishing marathons than there were *total* finishers in 1980! This is a defining social movement. The trend is obvious, and the numbers continue to increase at exciting rates.

What's behind this phenomenon? Running or walking 26.2 miles is not natural. The effort expended is significant. Runners and walkers alike, when asked how they feel at the finish of a marathon, will tell you, "It felt like 26.2 miles."

What we have witnessed in the last several decades is more than just the growth of a sport. Distance running and walking are now among the most popular sports in the country. Why? After all, the distances haven't gotten any shorter or easier. So why do the numbers continue to grow?

There are several contributing factors. One is that nearly all who run or walk these long distances do so to increase their endurance (stamina). Running and walking are simple exercises that make people feel stronger and better equipped to handle the sometimes exhausting pace of their daily lives.

Two, running and walking are ideal recreational activities for time-pressed, efficiency-seeking people. You can meet new people and strengthen existing relationships while walking and running at a conversational pace—the pace recommended by sports docs for maximum cardiovascular benefits.

Three, running and walking are opportunities for fund-raising for worthy causes. The Leukemia & Lymphoma Society and other charities have developed training programs that enable runners and walkers to raise funds for finishing a race. In return, they may receive a free trip to the event, including airfare, hotel expenses, and race registration fees, plus a training coach. These runners are often motivated by a desire to do good in the world. I've talked with runners who are running in support of someone struggling with cancer, and they say, "If my friend can go through *that*, the least I can do is try to complete a marathon to help." As they train, they get hooked on the activity, the camaraderie, and the chance to help make a difference, and they go back and spread the word to others.

Four, races provide entertainment. As previously noted, races such as the Rock 'n' Roll Marathon series provide music stages at every mile, cheerleading competitions along the course, and a huge concert party at the end of the day. These races are very lively events.

Five, with more people interested in going the distance, there has been an increase in training programs and greater responsiveness to beginners. Many running clubs now have coaches to work specifically with beginning runners and walkers.

Admittedly, this huge explosion in endurance training and racing might never have happened if the sport hadn't received one special down-to-earth celebrity endorsement. This shot in the arm came from Oprah Winfrey running in the 1994 Marine Corps Marathon in Washington, DC, as part of her nationally publicized personal health and weight loss campaign. Oprah opened the door for all those "non-athletes" who either thought the achievement was beyond their physical capability or felt too intimidated to try. Oprah tried it and did it, and the rest followed. Among my own patients are several dozen who have told me that Oprah made the difference.

The world is running or walking for exercise. Everybody is doing it and for good reason. All you need is a pair of running shoes; there is no extra equipment, no club or green fees, no renting a court, no need for a teammate. The statistics are astounding: In 2007, the running shoe industry sold more than 1 billion pairs of running shoes.

At the most recent Running USA convention, attendees learned that runners number in the tens of millions and they are a diverse, well-educated, and, above all, committed group:

- There are upward of 75 million total runners in the United States (includes all levels and abilities); 53 percent of these runners are male, and 47 percent are female.
- 94 percent are college educated.
- 93 percent run at least 3 days per week, 64 percent at least 4 days per week, and 35 percent 5 or more days per week.
- 64 percent have finished at least 1 marathon, 33 percent have finished at least 4 marathons, and 17 percent have finished 10 or more marathons.
- In the course of a year, they purchase an average of 2.9 pairs of running shoes, and 17 percent buy their running shoes online.

These runners have one overriding concern: They want to keep running. Their biggest worry is that they will get injured so that they cannot train, cannot exercise, and will lose the aerobic health and fitness that they worked so hard to achieve! They will even avoid going to the doctor for fear that he or she will tell them to stop. By the time they get there, the condition or injury is so far along that they face a long layoff from the sport they love.

What are all these runners or walkers missing? Just as you raised your child and picked up *Dr. Spock's Baby and Child Care* for every issue you encountered, runners and walkers need a handy manual telling them about every ache, pain, condition, and injury they may encounter. They need to know when to see a doctor, when they can treat an injury on their own, how to enter a race, what to expect, and how to maximize the experience.

This is what I have done with *Running Doc's Guide to Healthy Running*: It will fill your void; it's a *Dr. Spock* for every runner. Carry this

My First Marathon: A Major Lesson!

I grew up a sports fan. As far back as I can remember, I was playing or watching ball. As a child, I went to bed with the radio under my pillow, listening to games. I'd hear Marv Albert calling, "DeBusschere to the top of the key, YES!" and I'd yell, "YES!" and get into trouble.

After school I played touch football, or basketball in my driveway, but I thought of myself as a swimmer, swimming four to five days a week, even at age 10. I was encouraged to go AAU at 12 but decided that my studies and my interest in medicine (even at that age) would not allow the training I would need to do. At Rolling Hills Day Camp on Long Island I was the top swimmer and progressed to swim counselor, Red Cross Water Safety Instructor, Nassau County lifeguard, and, finally, pool director at camp. Did I think of running? No way! It looked boring.

Throughout my time at Lafayette College I continued to swim four to five days a week and play Frisbee football before dinner on the beautiful quad in the center of campus. Watching ball, I always focused in as players got hurt, and I watched the team physician on TV assessing the injury. Did I watch running events on TV? No way! Boring!

So when I went off to Emory Medical School, I had truly decided I would be a sports physician to combine my love for sports and for medicine. One day while walking on campus with my classmates, we saw a sign: "Run the Atlanta Marathon Thanksgiving Day. Get a turkey." Being medical students, my new friends immediately jumped in. "OK, Sports Doc, get us a turkey." Being in good shape from all that swimming, I thought, "How tough can this be?" and signed up.

Emory had a great pool, so I did what any naive sports doc in training might wrongly do: I upped my mileage in the pool! I was aerobically trained, so how could I go wrong? I swam five days a week for five months and thought I was ready.

continues

My First Marathon, continued

Picture this: I looked good! New shirt and shorts, new socks, and beautiful new running shoes. I had had my hair cut two days prior. I was ready for the post-race pictures. Race morning I had a bagel with peanut butter and banana and drank some orange juice. I was ready!

Then . . . the gun went off. All these runners took off, and there I went. In the first mile I said to myself, "Wait a minute; I can't glide." So much for the swim training. I went out in that first mile at a 12-minute pace and slowed down from there! By the time I finished—and I did finish—I was walking, and I finished a well-documented dead last. They were taking the clocks down. I was chafed in places I hadn't known existed, places that we hadn't studied yet in gross anatomy class! When I crossed the finish line, my friends were relieved because they had been calling the local emergency rooms. The operational personnel were yelling, "Keep walking!" I yelled back, "I paid for 26.2, not an inch further." And they had run out of turkeys!

I learned some very important lessons that day. And later on, when professors talked about these lessons in sports medicine classes, I could totally relate:

1. Always train in the sports you intend to compete in. Seems simple now, but boy was I surprised that day.
2. Respect the distance. A marathon (or even a half-marathon) is not a walk around the block. It requires training for a runner to finish healthy and feel great.
3. Don't do anything new on race weekend. This is now my mantra to all my patients. When I speak to newbies, I get reminded daily of all that new stuff I did. What a mistake.

So please don't be like me and think you know how to do something without asking people who do know. My hope is that this book will help you. Believe me, you don't want to skip the section on chafing!

manual, be informed about what to ask your doctor, and use it to help understand what your doctor is telling you.

The Marathon, Then and Now

Marathons have been around for a long time—since 490 B.C., to be exact, when Phidippides, a Grecian messenger, ran approximately 25 miles from Marathon to Athens to deliver the news that the Athenian army had defeated the Persians. According to legend, Phidippides arrived totally exhausted, delivered the news, and promptly expired. He was therefore not only history's first recorded marathoner, but also history's first recorded marathon casualty. Today, we handle medical emergencies with far greater success.

When the Olympic Games were revived in 1896, Michel Breal, working at the Sorbonne, decided to have a race commemorating the Phidippides legend: again, a 25-mile (more or less) contest from Marathon to Athens. So at 2:00 P.M. on April 10, 1896, which was the fifth and final day of these revived Olympic Games, 25 runners stood at the starting line at the Battle of Marathon's warrior tomb in Athens. Some 100,000 spectators lined the road, many holding wine and bread for the runners. After a remarkably fast 2 hours, 58 minutes, and 50 seconds, a 23-year-old fellow named Spiridon Louis of Greece won, 7 minutes ahead of the next fastest runner.

The now-official marathon distance became established at 26 miles and 385 yards at the 1908 Olympics in London, simply because the royal family wanted the race to start at Windsor Castle and finish in front of the king and queen's royal box at the Olympic stadium. This distance is almost precisely 42 kilometers, and it has remained the standard ever since.

The marathon "foothold" in the United States goes back to the Boston Athletic Association Marathon, started in 1897, which remains the oldest continually held marathon in this country.

In the intervening years, the marathon has captured the imagination of millions around the world who see it as the ultimate test of human endurance. In 1948, during the first Olympic Games after World War II, held in London, Belgian runner Etienne Gailly, running his first marathon, was the first to arrive at the stadium, but he still had 400 meters to go. Gailly fell, exhausted, in front of the crowd. Showing enormous heart, he got up, fell again, and then staggered toward the finish line, encouraged by the cheering crowd. Though Gailly was passed by two competitors, he was still satisfied with the bronze medal. After all, he had indeed accomplished his goal of finishing the race! That feeling of accomplishment from simply finishing is what the vast majority of marathoners and half-marathoners seek.

Since the 1980s, many cities throughout the world have begun holding their own marathons. More recently, many have expanded to offer a category for walkers—though plenty of marathons remain committed solely to runners. And half-marathons have sprung up as a long-distance race for beginners or for those who have not trained for the full distance.

At the 2005 ING New York City Marathon, a 37-year-old man stopped at the 24th-mile medical station. He had flown from Greece to run in New York City. He looked pale, and every part of his body hurt. When asked by the medical team what was wrong, he replied, "Phidippides died one mile too far."

I cannot promise you that you will never curse Phidippides at some point during your long-distance training or the race itself. But I do guarantee that if you keep this book with you as you train and prepare to race, and absorb its messages and do your best to follow the advice, you'll have the tools to carry on in the face of any temptation you might feel to stop.

Marathon and Postmarathon Physiology

I know that the word *physiology* sounds scary to a lot of people, as helpful as a chalkboard full of calculus notes. And, yes, back in basic biology class, all those body systems making who-knew-what chemicals so that the human organism could run itself were pretty intimidating to me, too.

But marathon physiology does not need to be complicated. First, you have a vested interest in *this* physiology because this time the physiology is about *you*. And second, understanding basic physiological principles will make it easier for you to cope with and adjust to what your body does during long endurance events. So follow along. This is not rocket science, but it could help turn you into a rocket!

Not Just a Run Around the Block!

During an endurance event or a long training run or walk (longer than 10 kilometers), the blood vessels in the legs become dilated to enhance blood flow to and from the leg muscles. Similarly, more blood goes to the skin to enhance cooling. This naturally takes blood away from the gut, the kidneys, and, to a lesser extent, the brain.

After exercise stops, these vessels temporarily maintain their dilated state. But when exercise ceases, there is also a loss of the "pumping action" of the muscles, a process that helps return blood to the heart. These factors together result in blood pooling in the lower extremities. That's why, after you finish running or walking a long distance, you need to "warm down" by walking for at least 10 minutes (15 minutes or more is even better). This walking will allow the pumping action of the lower extremity muscles to continue, pushing blood back to your heart, gut, kidneys, and brain and assisting you in "equilibrating" back to your normal physiology.

Now you know why finish lines and family reunion areas at endurance events are set up so that you have to walk and can't just stop cold. It's done to help you recover. So just keep walking. You will feel better for it! (Of course, if you need medical assistance in the finish area, it will be there for you.)

Exercise-Associated Collapse

The most common reason for exercise-associated collapse after the finish of a long-distance event is blood pooling in the legs, which is formally known as postural hypotension. The longer the race is, the greater is the risk of exercise-associated collapse.

Several factors contribute to the development of postural hypotension. When you stand around after a race or long run instead of walking, blood collects in your legs, decreasing the amount available to your brain and abdominal organs, and syncope (a "blackout") can result. Some people will experience warning signs, such as lightheadedness, nausea, and visual disturbance, prior to syncope. Others won't.

We've all seen one consequence of this diversion of blood flow in the sorry spectacle of runners throwing up after trying to drink just after finishing a hard run or race. The blood has not yet equilibrated to the internal organs, including the stomach, so food and liquid are not moving with normal peristaltic movements (peristalsis is the waves of contraction in your throat when you swallow, or in your intestine as your digestive system does its duty, moving food and drink through your body). When you try to put something in that empty, essentially nonfunctioning gut, the stomach rejects it, and the food or drink ends up on your shoes instead of in a more useful place.

If you do suffer from collapse or syncope, remember that you should drink fluids only after you are up and walking again. Blood flow, remember, has to return to the gut so that the fluids travel in the proper direction!

Running Doc's 20-Minute Protocol

The initial treatment for any person who can't continue to walk after an endurance event and equilibrate blood flow aided by the natural pumping of the leg muscles is to do what has been called "Running Doc's 20-Minute Protocol." First the finisher is helped to lie down with the legs elevated. A folding chair is useful with the person's back flat on the ground, upper legs at a right angle upward, knees bent 90 degrees, and the lower legs lying comfortably on the seat of the chair. Icing down (or using cool water on) the legs comes next, along with massaging the legs with a kneading action back in the direction of the heart.

The athlete will usually come around in a few seconds and feel better within a few minutes. Once awake and alert, the participant will be raised to a sitting and then a standing position in gradual stages over the next 15 to 20 minutes: first lowering the legs, then sitting up on the ground, then sitting in the chair with the legs dangling, and finally standing and walking with assistance.

Figure II.1

20-Minute Protocol

If this doesn't work within 20 minutes, something else is going on and transport to a hospital is usually recommended. But fortunately, this protocol almost always works, and very few people who collapse after an endurance event ever need transport or hospitalization.

When the Protocol Doesn't Work

In the rare case of a person who doesn't respond to this conservative treatment, there is likely a more serious underlying medical condition, such as hyponatremia (low sodium volume in the blood). This person should have a more in-depth evaluation. Usually, the medical personnel at the scene will determine the need for further evaluation. Should they ask you to go to a hospital to have your electrolytes checked (blood sodium, potassium, etc.), don't be afraid to go. They are doing their best for you, and you may need only some extra medical help to assist you on your way to a rapid recovery.

An interesting diagnostic point is whether collapse occurred before or after the runner reached the finish line. If the collapse happened before the finish, it is likely the result of an identifiable medical problem that developed (heat stroke, hyponatremia, etc.). If the collapse occurred after the finish line, it is likely due to the athlete's marathon physiology (blood pooling in the legs), and the patient will likely respond to the previously discussed treatments within 20 to 30 minutes.

IV Fluids

Recent research has definitively shown that intravenous (IV) fluids do not speed or enhance the recovery of marathon participants. Fluids by mouth are preferred, and athletes do better faster if they drink properly. Follow the fluid guidelines for recovery. In fact, we now know that it may actually be harmful to administer IV fluids to a person without knowing his or her serum electrolytes. If your serum sodium is too low, for example, and you get the wrong fluid, you can experience seizures or worse.

At all marathons I am associated with, if a physician decides a patient needs an IV, I insist that the patient also needs the care of an emergency room where proper monitoring and blood tests can be done. So on my watch, if a runner needs an IV, he or she also receives an ambulance trip to the nearest hospital. Certainly, I do have IVs available on-site in the rare instance that someone is in distress (heart attack, severe heat stroke, etc.), but I do not allow them to be used as a matter of course.

What's the point of telling you all this about how I run my medical tents? Just to drive the point home that there's nothing better than drinking appropriately before, during, and after your marathon. See Part I for complete hydration guidelines in training and on race day.

The 10 Commandments of Marathon Running

There's nothing common about common sense. If there were, endurance athletes wouldn't have to be reminded of the most basic precautions to keep from hurting themselves.

But they do need to be reminded, especially when so many potential marathoners pour all the training and racing of their yearlong preparation into one big, final blowout of a race. The morning after, I can count on a stream of telephone calls from patients who either can't figure out what went wrong or just need to admit to some blunder. Smart people, apparently, make mistakes all the time.

In fact, every physician who has ever covered a marathon, including me, has seen far too many of these people hunched disconsolately in our medical tents after a slipup they thought they were too savvy to make. As a result, the International Marathon Medical Directors Association (IMMDA) began keeping a list of what goes wrong most often. Yes, at one point I'd have said some of the resulting 10 Commandments were too elementary for athletes who'd been around the block a few times. But that was before I saw who was filling up the medical tents. The commandments are for marathoners in particular, but they apply to any endurance sport where you're about to lay it on a tougher line than you have in a while.

1. **Make sure you're physically fit for the activity you're undertaking.** That means more than doing the training mileage.

You're about to take a car that usually goes for groceries and drive it to Florida, and you don't want sudden mechanical surprises from previously hidden problems. Runners, for example, should be aware of pronated feet, high-arched ankles, bowed legs, or leg-length discrepancies. Physical characteristics like these are more likely to cause injuries in endurance events than during training. So if you're going where you've never gone before, either in distance or in pace, consider a good exam by a sports medicine physician before you toe the line. That is not to say you must get these things corrected if you are in no pain (if it's not broke, don't fix it!). It is to be aware of them so that if you do get some pain, you know there is something biomechanical being magnified by each step as you increase your mileage.

2. **Train properly.** Too obvious for words? Maybe, if you've been following a training plan designed for you. But if you're coming to the line with a workout log peppered with the "workouts of champions," you may be closer to my waiting room than you are to the winner's circle. Select and follow a training plan that is appropriate for your skill level, experience, and the race distance.

3. **Follow guidelines for proper nutrition.** Most athletes already know that carbohydrates and fats are the body's main race fuels, but what about protein for muscles? Don't worry. In a balanced diet you're getting plenty, and any extra doesn't become muscle anyway; it becomes fat. Worse yet, a body with excess protein has to use extra water to eliminate nitrogen by-products, and in a long race there's no such thing as extra water. And as for that plate full of pasta before the event, if you don't normally eat pasta in heaping piles, don't start now. For more details and recommendations regarding eating before and around your endurance event, follow my guidelines in Part I.

4. **Maintain adequate hydration.** Everyday marathoners aren't the only skeptics about the virtues of water stops. I see professional runners skipping them, figuring, "Hey, I'm making

such good time, so why slow down?" But they are slowing down anyway—from dehydration. Learn to drink when you are thirsty and you will do fine.

Sports drinks work best, but this is no time to experiment. If you haven't tried them in training, don't start now. As unlikely as it seems, those friendly carbohydrates your muscles crave can instead irritate a surprised stomach and cause cramps, especially if the carbohydrates are from something you are not used to. Again, for further guidelines and suggestions, see Part I.

5. **Warm up on race day, and stretch every day.** Stretching is especially important for marathoners. Global flexibility makes for more enjoyable runs and walks. Never stretch a "cold" muscle; always warm up *before* stretching. Make sure you stretch every day.

On race day do a 10- to 15-minute warm-up. Light jogging, jumping jacks, anything that makes you warm. Do not stretch before the event.

And once you're across the finish line, don't just quit in happy exhaustion. Your tight muscles are now riddled with little microtears, and if you don't stretch again, they're going to heal at a shorter length. The whole muscle will end up smaller, and the next time you work it hard, you will pull something. So lightly stretch the same way you do in training, no more and no less. Remember, nothing new on race day!

6. **Dress according to the weather.** Simple? Not always, especially for a late fall event. You may need to layer on some throwaway clothes so that you're warm until the start; once you're cool enough after the race begins, you can toss these clothes aside. Because cotton socks hold your sweat, try one of the more specialized running socks you can get at a local running store. The wicking away of moisture from the skin that the synthetic fabrics in these socks can achieve may prevent those nasty blisters you'll otherwise have at the end!

7. **Use proper, comfortable running shoes.** The people I've treated for bloody feet, black toenails, and blisters invariably had new shoes. Believe me, no matter what you read, shoes must be broken in. Even the same model you've always worn can have mild imperfections or something in one shoe that's not in the other. Nothing's always on the money.

   If you're buying a new pair, do it in the afternoon or evening when your feet are swollen, and do it weeks before running in them so that you can walk around and test them out. Then break them in during the weeks before the event so that you are not toeing the start line in brand-new shoes.

8. **Watch the condition of the surface.** Race directors try to give you a safe ride, but there will always be enough holes, oil slicks, or misplaced hazard markers to keep my ankle-mending business going. Try not to become part of it.

9. **Go at your own pace.** Even race winners know this. The championship swimmers I treat tell me that if they're swimming to beat whoever's in the next lane instead of themselves, they rarely do their best. And they usually pull something or get hurt trying to overextend what their body is ready to do.

10. **Listen to your body.** If you feel sick, you probably are. Stop. But what about a pain? Here's my rule: If it changes your mechanics—your normal running or walking form—stop. But if you can slow down and hold on to your form, you can probably finish the race safely.

Basic stuff, but any medical team member will tell you this: If you don't break the 10 Commandments, you probably won't break yourself either.

And remember the cardinal rule above all: Do nothing new on race day. If you stick with what you've been doing, chances are you will finish feeling the best you can, accomplished, and ready for your next race.

PART III
RUNNING DOC'S REPAIR SHOP

Running Doc's Repair Shop

Injury Prevention and Treatment Strategies

Like it or not, the reality is that somewhere along the buildup to a race, during the training period or in the race itself, you will have a physical problem that needs to be addressed. The problem will most likely take the form of an overuse injury—usually the end result of constant repetition of some biomechanical disadvantage you may have in your feet or some quirk you may have in your stride. But if you understand ahead of time how overuse injuries occur, you may be able to head off problems to come. For example, you may need an orthotic (an arch support that controls abnormal foot motion) to help prevent these injuries. The time to get orthotics is before the damage occurs, so that they can prevent it.

Understanding injuries common in marathoners will also help you be an educated consumer if you do need to see your doctor and will help both you and your doctor to minimize your downtime. Few injuries—other than fractures or stress fractures—require you to stop running. But if you've got to stop for a while, I'll show you how best to keep active with other sports so that you won't become detrained and you'll be able to get back to your full training program as soon as you realistically can.

J. Willis Hurst and Coca-Cola

As I worked on this book and thought about how I should proceed to fill you in on injuries and conditions, I knew that diagnosing your specific problem at long distance would be almost impossible. I certainly can discuss injuries and conditions in this guide and give you the most current information on how to prevent, treat, and recover from them so that when you see your physician, you can be better informed and know if you are getting the right answer or the brushoff. But for diagnosis? You need to see your own doctor, in person.

This may seem like a contradiction—after all, this is a medical guide—so let me explain the distinction further. When I was thinking about how to begin this project, I asked myself a number of questions, with these most prominent: How could I get everyone interested in communicating with a doctor? And how could I get you, dear reader, to think "medically" instead of turning to the old wives' tales treatments that are so common to all athletic pursuits, including running? A story from my medical school days came to mind.

I was born in New York City but decided to go to medical school at Emory in Atlanta because a physician there named J. Willis Hurst, MD (famous for writing the book *The Heart*, which you will find on all cardiologists' shelves), taught the "clinical methods" course. Dr. Hurst is still well-known as the "modern-day William Harvey" (the famous English physician who in 1628 published a landmark book on the circulation of the blood), and he offered the course that, as he put it, "would teach us which end of the stethoscope to put in our ears." You can imagine my excitement on the first day of this course, second year of medical school, as the entire class of 125 students sat in the Grady Hospital auditorium waiting for this man.

J. Willis arrived five minutes late. He walked down the center aisle from the back. He was a short, white-haired man, hair disheveled, wearing a white coat that looked like it hadn't been ironed since Reconstruction days. When he got to the stage, he faced his audience and with a Jimmy Carter smile said in a very heavy southern drawl, "Good mornin'."

He continued, "I woke up this morning and I asked myself the question, How many Coca-Cola signs are there between my breakfast room and the Grady auditorium?

"I then proceeded to wash up, shower, and had my Special K with skim milk and some sliced banana for potassium in 27 spoonfuls. I then drank my fresh squeezed orange juice with a tweak of fresh squeezed grapefruit juice, 'cause I like the twang, in 12 sips. I then tied my tie in a Windsor knot. . . . It took three times to do it to get these ends of the tie placed just right. I grabbed my briefcase, went to my car, got in, and started it up. It did take two turns of the ignition key to get it going since, as you know, today is a very chilly mornin'."

He then proceeded to tell us with graphic detail how he backed up the car, and then he described his route, step by step, mentioning every stop sign, traffic light, turn, and Coca-Cola sign. This went on for 45 minutes. Mind you, this was a 50-minute lecture, and he timed his story, which ended with his arrival at the Grady auditorium, to conclude just as the lecture period was drawing to the end.

He then said, "You see: There are four Coca-Cola signs between my breakfast room and the Grady auditorium."

Pause. Silence.

"I know; y'all think J. Willis here is either senile or on drugs!"

At this point we were all nodding yes and were totally confused.

"You see, my young colleagues, this is what medicine is all about. If I didn't ask myself 'How many Coca-Cola signs?' I couldn't now stand before you and tell you there are four."

We were all still lost until he then said, "If you don't ask yourself, 'Does this patient have the murmur of aortic stenosis?' you will never hear it. If you don't ask yourself, 'Does this patient have a posterior cruciate ligament tear?' you will never find it! Class dismissed. See you next week!"

This lecture had a greater effect on my practice than any other single thing in my life. If you ask the right questions, you can then come up with the right answers. The great doctors do not always know the answers, but the really smart ones know who, how, or where to get those answers.

Now it is our turn. Ask those questions. I will do my best to get you the answers you need or the information needed to ask intelligent questions to help point you in the correct direction. As we go through injuries, conditions, prevention, treatments, and race day strategies, you may not know the answer directly to your specific problems. But I am positive that you will be better informed so that you can ask the right questions of your specific doctor in order to get back to doing what you love most. I look forward to your using this book as your manual to help you stay in hot pursuit of your running/walking goals.

Nearly all the ailments described in this book have easy solutions to get you back on the road again safely and effectively. But you need to recognize when you can treat these ailments yourself and when you need help—and what kind of help. Fortunately, every condition comes with its own set of clues.

General Issues

As a sports doctor, I hear tons of questions about general medical issues that strike me as basic—basic not in the sense of simplistic, but in the sense that they are fundamental issues that I believe every endurance athlete should be familiar with. It is my intention in this section to anticipate questions that you may have and give you the answers at your fingertips. If I have missed something here (or elsewhere in the book), please write to me at runningdoc@competitorgroup.com. I will answer your question in my online column and also put it in the next edition of this book.

When Should a Runner Get a Physical Exam?

A middle-aged patient recently came to me nearly hysterical, having been told after her physical that everything was normal except for microscopic blood in her stool—something commonly tested for in people over 40. She was supposed to schedule herself for a battery of tests next: a gastrointestinal series and a colonoscopy. The blood in her stool might mean a tumor or just an ulcer, her doctor said, and she needed to find out which.

And a 50-year-old racewalker casually mentioned in the course of a sore Achilles exam that his internist thought he might have bladder cancer because of evidence of microscopic amounts of blood in his urine sample. Even though the rest of his physical had been fine, he was being sent for a bladder biopsy and an intravenous pyelogram (an X-ray of the kidney after injection of contrast fluid to visually define the body parts) to check his kidneys.

All it took to prove that they were both perfectly healthy were a couple of days of rest and an understanding of what happens to athletes' insides when they train hard. Six studies around the world have shown that about 5 percent of marathon-ready runners had evidence of microscopic gastrointestinal bleeding before the race. After the marathon it zoomed to 21 percent. The leading theory says that because up to 80 percent of the bowel's normal blood flow gets diverted to hardworking leg muscles during intense exercise, microscopic areas of oxygen-starved digestive-tract tissue could let blood seep through. All you do is take three days of rest and call the doctor on the fourth. If a retest is positive, it's time to get moving on additional procedures. But if it's negative, it was your workouts.

Same with "bladder cancer," which can be nothing more than exercise-induced hematuria (presence of blood in the urine). One in 5 marathoners has trace amounts of blood in the urine ("trace" meaning microscopic and not necessarily visible to the naked eye), and surveys show that 6 out of 10 football players seem to have the same thing. Again, how it gets there is speculative. We know that in long-distance running, the kidneys get short-changed by as much as 80 percent of their usual blood flow, damaging a small number of cells enough that they leak. But it doesn't take something like a marathon to bring the condition on, and in shorter distances it may simply be a problem with the bladder, which injures itself as its parts flap together.

Both conditions are harmless, but because they are easily mistaken for illnesses that are not, being told you have them can do serious damage to your mind—not to mention your wallet. Taking 72 hours off from all physical activity before your exam should eliminate the confusion.

Should You Stretch?

You may or may not think that stretching is very important. After all, as I explain later, stretching before exercise has largely been discredited as an injury preventer. However, I am here to tell you that stretching is indeed very important when done properly and conscientiously.

Clearly, being more flexible—which stretching encourages—allows the body to "ignore" some biomechanical imperfections, which helps to prevent injury or chronic inflammation by rubbing. The question is, how do you get to this flexible state? As you know, being Gumby-like is a factor of heredity; some people who have done little stretching can contort in all types of positions, whereas others need to work at improving their range of motion.

A global stretching program has been shown to be the answer. Followed by a brief warm-up to raise your body temperature one-half degree (as evidenced by a minimal sweat), your muscles become more pliable and stretch more easily. When you fit in a stretch routine is up to you, but the key is to stretch daily. Time of day is of no consequence; doing it is. Meet with a personal trainer or coach to go over which stretches to do and the proper technique you need to do them.

Stretching before you run is *not* necessary because it has been proven not to decrease injury. Yes, warm-up is important for getting blood flow and warmth to your muscles, but if you are globally flexible, that additional stretch before the run does nothing for you. Stretching after the run, however, is a good practice because it helps maintain the length of the muscle/tendon unit after that unit has been stretched with exercise.

Orthotics: What They Are, When You Need Them, and Where to Get Them

Most sports medicine physicians use the term *orthotic* to describe a custom foot support that is made using a cast or impression of the foot that is then "corrected" so that foot and lower leg alignment is artificially maintained when the device is worn. Orthotics are required when there is a significant malalignment of the foot or lower leg leading to injury. Just as with children's building blocks, if you are off at the bottom, something above may be out of whack, which in the case of your body means that it can lead to injury.

The design of an orthotic is what determines its overall effectiveness. There are two major design factors that we should look at. The first is the material used in the construction, and the second is the length and shape of the orthotic.

Materials that are used to construct orthotics can be flexible, semiflexible, semirigid, or rigid. For running, flexible or semiflexible materials work the best by far. Although some practitioners prefer to use more rigid materials, my experience has taught me that more flexible materials are incredibly superior. Although it is true that flexible or semiflexible materials are less durable, their shorter lifespan pales in comparison to the better performance they achieve. Materials such as leather, cork, moldable rubbers, foams, and lightweight aerated plastics make excellent orthotics for runners. These materials are shaped over plaster impressions of the feet and then corrected by the use of posts (especially forefoot posts in overpronators, or folks who roll their feet inward excessively) to align the foot, ankle, and lower leg. With minimal maintenance, orthotics made from these materials can last five years.

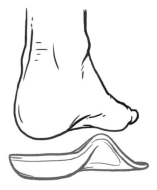

Figure III.1

Orthotic

To understand why the length and shape of an orthotic are important, runners and walkers must be aware of the demands that exercise places on the foot. The job of an orthotic starts with the initiation of the running cycle as the heel of one foot contacts the ground. The orthotic then needs to guide the foot and lower leg into the proper angle of contact to allow shock absorption and slow leg rotation. This is accomplished by heel positioning on the inside of the orthotic and the depth of the heel cup. This phase of running lasts for only a split second, so orthotics that are based on, or designed for, "heel control" are totally inefficient and ineffective in runners. The faster a runner runs, the more ineffective such orthotics become as the heel contact phase shortens.

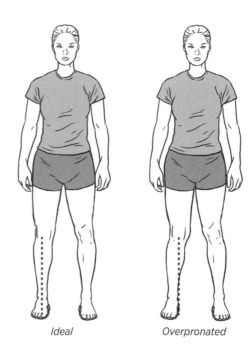

Figure III.2A

Checking orthotic alignment   *Ideal*   *Overpronated*

Next, the running foot pronates (rolls inwardly) to absorb shock. Orthotics are designed to allow normal pronation but to limit abnormal pronation (overpronation). The entire orthotic is involved in limiting pronation. To accomplish this, the orthotic must contour to the runner's foot. Any gap between the orthotic and the foot may allow foot deformation, excessive rubbing and blisters, and overpronation leading to injury higher up above the foot, all the way to the back (as with children's building blocks, if you don't have a stable base, the top of the pile will be wobbly).

Finally, during the push-off phase of running, the orthotic must guide the running foot up onto the metatarsals (the forefoot) and allow normal supination (outward roll) to occur. Orthotics that end behind the metatarsal heads (i.e., short of the ball of the foot) do not accomplish this task as well as full-length orthotics (those that are posted/angulated through the ball of the foot). This last point is very, very important. Orthotics that end behind the metatarsals are 30 to 40 percent less efficient in runners and walkers, and I can vouch for this in my practice because short orthotics are the ones I am most likely to see in my office when a patient comes in with a running or walking injury and emphatically insists that he or she has orthotics! When I switch these patients to full-length orthotics, the problem is usually corrected and does not come back.

When orthotics are working poorly, the reason is usually traced to improper usage. An orthotic can work only when it is worn. Some runners use their devices so infrequently that they can never perform properly. Some types of running problems in certain runners require the devices to be used whenever the athlete bears weight. Other problems in other runners may require use only while running or walking for endurance. A good rule of thumb is to start using your orthotics at all times until the problem subsides. Then gradually ease off the wearing time until you are comfortable with the amount of wear time or until your symptoms return.

Most patients ask me how they can know if their orthotics are wearing out or in need of refurbishing before the six-month checkup that I require. I recommend the following test: Take your orthotics out of your running shoes and stand in them with your feet shoulder-width apart. (You should stand out of your running shoes because we don't want the shoe structure to mask the effectiveness of the orthotic alone.) Keeping both heels on the ground, bend each knee, one at a time. When your knee is bent and you drop an imaginary perpendicular down from the kneecap (visualize this line from the front), it should land between the first and second toe, indicating that your biomechanics are well controlled. If your perpendicular comes out anywhere else, go get your orthotics checked!

Deciding whether you need orthotics depends on the shape of your foot and whether you are running or walking in pain. I regularly see patients in my office who say that they want orthotics but have no pain at all. You were born with the feet you have. Looking at them at rest and then again while running may tell you whether you are an overpronator or supinator, but if you have no pain or other issue, there is no need to correct the biomechanics. Be happy with your

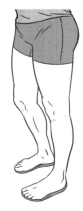

Figure III.2B
Checking orthotic alignment,
side view

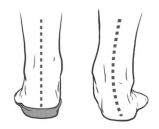

Figure III.2C
Checking orthotic alignment,
rear view

feet, and don't worry too much about what they look like when you run. When I was at the Virginia Beach Rock 'n' Roll Half Marathon expo, Frank Shorter came over to talk. While talking, he removed his running shoes to put on a new pair the sponsor had brought over. As soon as he removed his shoes, we saw the flattest overpronating feet possible. A local physical therapist sitting there could not help herself when she blurted out, "Holy mother of God!" Can you imagine that these feet ran and won marathons without any pain?

People reach what I call a "critical mass." When your body decides that a biomechanical disadvantage has been reached and you start to get pain, that is the time to consider, first, a more structured shoe and, second, an orthotic.

Who should make the orthotic, and is an over-the-counter orthotic a good one? Taking the second part of the question first, let me ask, which would you rather have: an over-the-counter eyeglass or your prescription? Or more pointedly, do you want an over-the-counter orthotic made from a simple impression of your foot, or do you want one that's made to fit your foot shape *and* to compensate for the off-kilter biomechanics that are causing your problem? I thought so.

And when a sports physician puts you facedown on an examining table, notes how your feet position themselves at rest, and measures your limbs, she or he is gathering information that will be just as important to the lab as your foot impression is. Some sports physicians will make a temporary device for you to wear for a week or two, as I do, to gather even more information about your foot positioning. What a sports physician should make for you should not be a Madame Tussaud's wax impression of your feet; it should be a device that when worn will make your biomechanics better.

Plenty of companies think sports medicine doctors should use the "you-do-it" mold kits they sell to produce quick-and-easy inserts that can probably help some patients. I don't buy that, and neither should you. You want the very best you can get, and that, of course, can come only from a professional whose life is devoted to getting patients past sports injuries. Knowing the injury helps fix the cause and prevent recurrence.

But please remember also that orthotics by themselves are almost never the whole cure. If you need them, you also need a shoe that they can work with; on their own, they don't do the job 100 percent. So if in fact you need orthotics, you will probably need a more structured shoe to go with them, which I am sure your sports physician will be discussing with you, as well as adequate stretching and strengthening!

When Can a Runner Donate Blood?

As the American Red Cross points out, every minute of every day someone needs blood. Donating blood is a selfless act of citizenship, and I encourage it—especially since, as the Red Cross notes, only 3 people out of every 100 in America donate regularly. If you have any question about whether you are eligible to donate, contact the Red Cross to clarify the situation. Blood donation centers also use the Red Cross criteria for who can and who cannot donate, and they can clear up any doubts in a jiffy.

Now, once you are cleared to donate, the question becomes, when should you donate? A donation equals approximately 1 pint of blood; the average adult body has 10 to 12 pints. The vast majority of people will not feel any different because of a donation. A very small percentage may experience temporary dizziness, but some rest and fluids will clear that up quickly. The body will replace the lost fluid within 24 hours.

But when running a marathon, you want everything as close to normal as possible. Therefore, I have the following suggestions:

- Never donate blood for the first time around a marathon. As you know, the first rule of marathoning is *do nothing new.* Although the general rule is 24 hours to recover, everyone reacts differently, and you need to know how you are going to feel after giving blood.
- If you know how your body reacts, the 24 hours feels right for you, and you must donate around marathon time, give yourself double the time suggested (i.e., 48 hours before a race) to recover.

- After the race, give yourself 48 hours as well to return yourself to a normal, hydrated state.

My gut feeling, however, is that I would never recommend donating blood around marathon time. There are plenty of other times during the year to do so when potentially decreasing your oxygen-carrying red blood cells won't matter. When you are running (or walking) 26.2 miles, you wouldn't want to risk decreasing those cells no matter what the medical literature says; it just makes good sense to be cautious.

Running and Cholesterol Levels

In 1991 I led a study on runners at the New York City Marathon and subsequently presented it at the American College of Sports Medicine's annual meeting. The results suggested that when it comes to total cholesterol count, not only is exercise good but also more exercise is better.

The news was in the "more." Although exercise had long been associated with good health, very little hard research had been done on the relationship between the amount of exercise and the degree of freedom from health risk factors, like high cholesterol. What if highly conditioned athletes, such as those prepared to run a marathon within a few days, could be tested and compared with fit but less highly conditioned subjects—in this case, the people who accompanied the marathoners to the number pickup exhibit hall?

So in this test, that's what we did. By race time we had tested more than 1,000 runners and "nonrunners" for total cholesterol. Runners were people going to the marathon starting line; nonrunners were all the others—not a sedentary group to be sure, but averaging a slower training pace and fewer weekly miles than the runners.

In order to test thousands of subjects, we had to stick with measuring total cholesterol rather than determining the more descriptive but time-consuming HDL and LDL values. Even so, it was apparent that all our subjects were well under the typical 200-plus total cholesterol count found in the general population and that the marathon runners had values lower still than their lesser-trained companions.

And we were hardly surprised to find that older subjects—runners and nonrunners alike—had higher cholesterol values than younger ones. Moreover, in three of the four groups, subjects who were heavier, and subjects who were heavier for their heights (higher weight/height ratios), also tended to have higher cholesterol.

The big exception was among the women prepared to run the marathon. For all practical purposes, their cholesterol levels had no statistical link to either their weights or their weight/height ratios! Older women did have reliably higher values, but poundage apparently had nothing to do with it. However, there are lots of possibilities for our finding, including the fact that we didn't separate pre- and postmenopausal women (estrogen levels drop after menopause, and estrogen is thought to have a protective role when it comes to cholesterol).

But one recommendation is incontrovertible from our study: *Keep exercising.* Healthier low total cholesterol profiles are unequivocally associated with some of the healthiest people among us: marathon runners and their friends.

So what about people with cholesterol levels 200 and above who eat "right" and exercise? Well, you just can't pick your parents! Heredity is the most important factor in your being able to get your level within a "good range." The new statin drugs like Lipitor and Crestor are excellent at controlling your cholesterol with minimal side effects. There have even been reports that they can eventually dissolve plaque that is already there. Given the proven increase in longevity with lower cholesterol, it just makes sense to use statins as you do your daily aspirin. I have found that the active runners among my patients tend to shy away from these drugs because they are sure their running takes care of it. *It doesn't!* So if your doctor suggests a statin, take it so that you can continue to run far and long for years to come.

Vitamin D

Vitamin D is important in maintaining organ systems and decreasing cancer risk. Vitamin D also helps regulate calcium and phosphorus absorption. It is made in the skin during exposure to sunlight.

Its deficiency in patients has been shown to result from inadequate intake of vitamin D in food, along with inadequate ultraviolet light exposure, disorders that limit its absorption (like "runner's trots"), kidney or liver disorders that impair conversion of vitamin D into its active form, and, rarely, a small number of hereditary disorders. Low levels of vitamin D can cause muscle cramps, spasms, osteoporosis (decreased bone mass), increased risk of infections, and increased risk of diseases like rickets and multiple sclerosis.

A dietary fact sheet from the National Institutes of Health tells us that natural sources of vitamin D include the following:

- Fish liver oils, such as cod liver oil
- Fatty fish species, such as herring, catfish, salmon, mackerel, sardines, tuna, and eel
- Whole eggs
- Beef liver
- Fortified milk products and cereals

I have found low vitamin D levels in my practice in patients who get side stitches and muscle cramps. Supplementation with 2,000 units per day cured their symptoms. (These people said they already *were* eating the recommended foods.)

My colleagues all agree that at this point we cannot pinpoint in everyone the cause of vitamin D deficiency. More research is being done to figure this out. My suggestion is that you ask to have your vitamin D level tested at your yearly physical, along with your other labs. If it is low, taking a simple vitamin each day may be necessary to bring up your level to a healthy one.

Aches and Pains

Frank Shorter, the gold medal winner of the marathon at the 1972 Summer Olympics, once said, "If you don't feel pain after completing an endurance event, you haven't gotten your money's worth." If Frank Shorter feels pain, then we all will feel pain. The question is, what can we do about these common aches that can crop up after a run? In this section, I aim to cover general, run-of-the-mill maladies. For diagnosis and treatment of more serious injuries, see the next section.

Acute Injury: Ice or Heat?

Although there appears to be a controversy about heat versus ice in the treatment of injuries and aches, there really isn't. Most health professionals who treat athletes on a regular basis agree that for the first 24 hours after a minor injury, ice is the treatment of choice. Heat tends to further injure friable (easily broken) blood vessel walls, thereby promoting leaking of fluid and increasing swelling. Ice, like heat, also vasodilates (widens the blood vessels), but unlike heat it does so without injuring the vessel walls, and, in fact, helps their integrity. Ice is truly a great vasodilator. Although initially vasoconstricting in the first few minutes, ice then deactivates the vasoconstrictors in the body and promotes and lengthens vasodilation and thus improves blood flow, as evidenced by the red area on the skin after icing.

After 24 hours we want to continue vasodilation to bring in blood, which carries nutrients and cells to promote healing. By now, the vessel walls have regained their integrity, and both ice and heat work: After a 20-minute treatment, both result in an area that looks red due to increased blood flow. Which should you use then? I still prefer ice because it temporarily deactivates receptors in the vessel walls (receptors are the types of cells that regulate blood flow to the area), thereby keeping the vessels open for an additional 45 minutes following a 20-minute treatment. When heat of any type is applied, as soon as the heat comes off, the vessel area begins to cool the receptors and the vessel walls are reactivated to normal blood flow. Therefore, ice gives you a longer treatment for a 20-minute application. Contrary to the conventional wisdom of switching back and forth between ice and heat, ice works better, three times a day for 20 to 30 minutes. Contrast baths of ice and heat find their main advantage not in inducing temperature swings, but in doing more treatment, and more treatment is always good to a point. You can ice up to six 20-minute treatments a day for most effect.

Be careful not to burn the skin with either treatment. My favorite way to ice is with a resealable plastic bag filled with ice and water, as opposed to using a frozen chemical pack sold for sports therapy, which can be too cold. With an ice and water mix, the water raises

Epsom Soaks: Yes or No?

There are a few misconceptions about Epsom salts that need to be cleared up. In my days back in medical school at Emory University, Dr. J. Willis Hurst, whom I often quote, addressed this very topic. There is no doubt, he said, that warm water soaks tend to make achy muscles feel better and help infections clear out and heal. However, patients tend to need a specific instruction from a doctor to do something, and simply telling them to put their extremities in warm water often isn't sufficiently "medical" to get them to follow through. Epsom salts thus became the magic prescription in the old days. In reality, Dr. Hurst said in his southern drawl, it was "just something to put the water in" so that the patients would do the soaks!

Epsom salts can be bought in any drugstore, over the counter, without a prescription. They are merely magnesium sulfite. Although some alternative-medicine types and others point to its medicinal curing effects, I have not read one good scientific study saying the substance actually does anything. And sure enough, when I have repeated the Dr. Hurst story to my patients to explain why they need a warm water soak (as for skin infections or tired, achy muscles), they usually smile and then follow through without the salt and feel better thanks to the pure warm water! (Thanks again, Dr. Hurst!)

Now, please don't use these soaks instead of ice baths immediately postexercise. Inflammation is like butter boiling in a pan. And sitting in warm water is like turning the heat up. Immediately after exercise, you want ice or cool water to cool down inflamed soft tissues. Warm soaks are good the day after for achy muscles and always good for infections.

I hope this clears things up. Epsom salts can't harm you (unless you are allergic), so if it makes you feel better to put something in the tub, be my guest. Just don't forget the warm water!

the temperature to 32 degrees so that there is no need for a cloth between the ice and the skin and no freezer burn to the skin. I have also found the common advice of using a bag of frozen peas useful, but just as with one of those chemical packs, frozen peas can get too cold, so take care to put a cloth between your skin and the pack.

Chafing

Areas that rub (between your thighs and under your armpits especially) may get irritated during repetitive movements while running or walking (or cycling and other similar activities). This is just irritated skin. To prevent, use some lube: petroleum jelly (Vaseline), BodyGlide, or whatever is handy.

If it is too late and you already are suffering from chafing, you must cleanse with soap and water; sometimes it is easiest to sit in a soapy bath. Then apply an antibiotic cream like Neosporin or Bacitracin twice a day.

If the area starts to weep fluid or gets red and warm, please see a doctor to be sure you are not getting infected. A short course of antibiotics may be needed to ward off infected skin.

Blisters

By far the most common ailment I see as a marathon medical director is blisters, especially after an event! The best way to avoid discomfort and time off from physical activities is to avoid getting blisters altogether (see below). But if blisters do surface, prompt treatment will get you back to form quickly and help prevent infection. Knowing what they are and how to prevent and treat them will help you help yourself.

Blisters form when the skin rubs against another surface, causing friction. First, a tear occurs within the upper layers of the skin (the epidermis), forming a space between the layers while leaving the surface intact. Once this occurs, watery fluid (serum) seeps into the space. Toes and the soles of the feet are most commonly affected, for several reasons. These areas often rub against running/walking shoes during physical activity, causing thicker and rather immobile epidermis. These conditions allow for the formation of blisters. In addition, blisters form more easily on warm, moist skin.

To prevent blisters, you need to minimize friction. For the feet, this begins with shoe selection. Shoes should fit comfortably, with approximately a thumb's width between your longest toe and the end of the shoe. Narrow shoes can cause blisters on the big toe and little toe. A shallow toe box can lead to blisters on the tops of the toes, and loose shoes can create blisters on the tips of the toes.

When shopping for new shoes, be sure to wear the same socks, insoles, or orthotics that you wear when training or racing. Try on new shoes in the evening because feet tend to swell during the day.

Walk or jog around the store to test for comfort before heading to the cash register, and then wear the new shoes around the house for a few hours to identify any areas of discomfort. It often helps to break in running or walking shoes by wearing them for two to three hours on the first day and gradually increasing use each day.

Socks can decrease friction between the feet and shoes. Socks made from polypropylene or other synthetics can wick moisture away from the skin more effectively than wool or cotton; these socks can be found at any sporting goods store.

Although you might find these synthetic socks at the next event expo you go to—maybe handed out for free in a goodie bag—trying a new type of sock on race day is not recommended. Take the freebies home and give them a try later, in training or just walking around. Then you'll know whether they work for you or not.

Layering your socks, or choosing double-layered socks, can minimize shearing forces and thus blisters. You can also carry extra pairs of socks to change into if your socks become too damp (especially if you have gone through a "spray station" on race day).

Another preventive measure is to use padded insoles (found at any supermarket or drugstore) to decrease friction in a specific area. Foot powders and spray antiperspirants that contain aluminum chlorhydrate or aluminum chloride also decrease moisture.

You can also apply a thin layer of petroleum jelly (Vaseline) to your feet before a race or other event to decrease friction. Conditioning the skin by gradually increasing activity tends to lead to the formation of protective calluses (thickened skin without any watery serum beneath) rather than blisters. I know—calluses are ugly, right? Well, they are not so bad, and better a callus that is always there and causes no trouble than a blister that bugs you for days.

If you get a blister, you'll want to relieve the pain, keep the blister from enlarging, and prevent infection. Specific steps depend on the size of the blister and whether or not it is intact. You can treat the vast majority of blisters yourself and need to call a doctor only if blisters become infected or recur frequently. Signs of infection you should be aware of include pus (a thick, milky white substance) draining from the blister and warm red skin around the blister and red streaks leading away from the blister.

Small, intact blisters that don't cause discomfort usually need no treatment. Nature's best protection against infection is a blister's own skin. Avoid the temptation to fuss with the blister; leave it alone! To protect the roof (the skin above the buildup of serum), this type of blister can be covered with a small adhesive bandage or Johnson & Johnson's "Blister Block" pads (found in supermarkets and pharmacies).

Larger or painful blisters that are intact should be drained without removing the skin. First, clean the blister with rubbing alcohol or soap and water. Then use a sharp, sterile object (a safety pin that you've boiled in water and washed with rubbing alcohol or a sterile lancet from a pharmacy) to punch a small hole at the edge of the blister. Drain the fluid with gentle pressure, and keep the area clean (using soap and water) and dry for 24 hours. Wear flip-flops. After 24 hours, you may then apply an antibiotic ointment such as Bacitracin or Neosporin and cover the blister area with a Band-Aid. Change the dressing daily—more frequently if it becomes wet, soiled, or loose.

Blisters with small tears should be treated the same way as those that you have punctured. Blisters with larger tears should be "unroofed" carefully with fine scissors (clip away the torn skin at the edge where it is attached), and the base should be cleansed thoroughly with soap and water or an antibacterial cleanser. Apply antibiotic ointment and bandages as described previously.

Bloody Nipples

Oh, do we all feel the pain when we see this! In fact, the most common spectator comment at finish lines is "Wow, that must hurt!" We all know it does. The good news is that this condition is easily prevented.

Nipple bleeding is most commonly seen in men, and it is a direct result of chafing against clothing, sweat, and salt. Nipples first become irritated and tender; then open wounds develop with bleeding. The raw skin and salt from sweat in these open wounds with a significant nerve supply are not comfortable in the least and take days to heal each time. Long-term scar tissue may develop from healing and rehealing, which will eventually make nipples less sensitive, something I'm sure you do not want! Fortunately, prevention is easy with these guidelines:

Dress properly. Wear soft, loose shirts; avoid a new, unwashed shirt. Instead of cotton, wear a synthetic sweat-wicking fabric as the base layer next to the skin. If the weather is warm enough, men can go topless. Please remember, however, that you need a sunblock as this method risks sunburn. Use a sunblock product that is waterproof so that your sweat doesn't wash it away. Don't fear not sweating; other areas without the sunblock are enough to allow your needed sweat mechanism.

Hydrate properly. We do not want you to run out of fluid; you need it to sweat. Without proper fluid, the sweat will dry up, leaving salt flakes that irritate. Do not drink too much or too little; use thirst as a guide. And check your urine. You want yours to look like lemonade. If it's clear, you are drinking too much; if it looks like iced tea, you are drinking too little.

Lube up (and/or cover up). Vaseline or generic petroleum jelly, BodyGlide, Band-Aids, and NipGuards all offer good prevention against rubbing.

Remove any nipple jewelry. Seems like a no-brainer, but I have seen participants who hadn't thought that their fashion statement was the cause behind their nipples' bleeding. An easy preworkout removal saves days of discomfort!

A short note to women smiling as they read this: You are *not* immune to nipple bleeding! Improper or poorly fitting sports bras are the cause. Avoid cotton, which keeps moisture in so that the soggy bra shifts back and forth; switch to a synthetic sweat-wicking fabric that pulls moisture away from the skin. And make sure your bra fits snugly, both in the band around your chest and the cup. If your bra is loose and moves, chances are it will cause chafing.

As a physician, I would be remiss if I didn't mention that if your nipples are bleeding but you have not chafed them, that is a time to see your doctor, as something more serious may be going on. If the problem is caused by chafing, however, following the preceding advice should alleviate this problem forever.

Lacerations and Abrasions

Cuts and scrapes need to be cleaned with soapy water, coated with an antibiotic cream, and protected with a bandage. If you look at the cut and the skin is broken enough for you to see fat globules (they look like little white bulbs of Jell-O), then a trip to an ER is essential within the first four hours so that the laceration can get stitches; after four hours, most doctors will not stitch it for fear of infection. So if you want less of a scar, get to that ER.

In either case, if the area starts to weep fluid or gets red and/or warm, seek medical attention right away. The cut may be getting infected, and you may need an antibiotic by mouth.

Colds, Flu, and Marathon Sniffles

It is well-known that moderate exercise boosts immunity. ("Moderate" exercise means about 30 minutes per day.) Even though average adults are constantly exposed to viruses, they generally have only two or three colds or upper respiratory infections per year.

Marathoners and triathletes fall into a category of "too much exercise" (I hate that term, by the way), where, after intense, prolonged exercise, immunity is actually decreased for up to 72 hours postevent. During this time, the athlete is more susceptible to illness—including, yes, colds and the flu, but much more commonly the "marathon sniffles," which is a cold that occurs as mileage increases toward the end of marathon training or within 72 hours of finishing an endurance race.

Can you run with these? The general rule is, if the illness is above the throat and there is no fever present (nothing over 101 degrees without the use of acetaminophen [Tylenol] or ibuprofen), then you are safe to run. If below the throat, in the chest, or requiring medication to keep the fever down, that is the time to rest and allow your body to get well. Fever plus the natural temperature elevation associated with running may cause damage to vital internal organs and is not to be ignored. Besides endurance running/walking, other risk factors for decreased immune function include older age, smoking, overtraining, stress, poor nutrition, and lack of rest.

So what can you do to help avoid colds and flu when your immunity is low? Besides the obvious guidelines of staying away from sick people as well as eating well and getting proper rest, I suggest getting checked as soon as symptoms start. Certain medications may be appropriate for you. Wash your hands or use alcohol-based hand cleansers as frequently as you can. When you greet people, don't exchange kisses and try not to shake hands. And, of course, to protect others, if you develop symptoms, try to use tissues to wipe your nose and cover your mouth (and please throw the tissues in the trash; do not leave them lying around). Use an antibacterial cleanser frequently (spray or wipe) on telephones, computer keyboards, and workspaces where germs can linger.

And *please* don't stop participating in running or walking events, including marathons, just because your immune system gets taxed for 72 hours afterward. It comes back strong and healthy, as you do. Just be smart the three days postevent (eat well and get some rest to recover) to prevent catching something you might have normally fought off.

The Common Cold

Everyone who suffers from a cold, with all the stuffy mucus, tons of Kleenex, raw nose, weepy eyes, headache, sneezing, coughing, and stopped ears, asks the same questions: Which cold medicine do I take? And how do I cure this thing? Unfortunately, the answers are not simple. If there were a "cure" for the common cold, there would be no confusion about treatment and someone would have already won the Nobel Prize.

The best analogy I've heard about the common cold came from a good ol' country doctor in Georgia where I went to medical school. Dr. H. Kenneth Walker said on rounds one morning that a cold is like a dirty driveway. The dirt is the viral "bugs" that cause your cold, and your mucus is the high-powered hose you use to clean the dirt off. If you drink more fluids, the hose pushes a stronger stream of water and the driveway clears faster (as does the cold). If you take those over-the-counter meds that dry you up and make you feel better, it is like putting chocolate pudding through that hose: It lengthens the time needed to clean that driveway. So it is really your choice: Feel better but withstand it longer, or tough it out for a shorter period of time.

I am sure people will write to me with their thoughts on zinc, echinacea, vitamins, and so on as preventing or shortening colds. Although there are anecdotal reports of these "cures," physicians always base their recommendations on reproducible scientific studies published in reliable and peer-reviewed medical journals. Journal-reviewed studies do not exist for these types of "cures." They are reasonably safe when not used to excess, however, so you can take them if you want. But there are no doctor guarantees on these!

You can run with a head cold. If you develop a fever, however, then you need to stop running and see a doctor. Colds don't usually have a fever. A fever may indicate a bacterial infection on top of the viral infection, which would call for an antibiotic. Running elevates your body temperature, so running with a fever where your temperature would be elevated even further could put you at risk for a heat illness, so please refrain. An antifever med like Tylenol is not enough to control this risk.

And I would be remiss if I didn't mention chicken soup. All of our grandmas have at one time told us of this age-old remedy. The good news here is that my great-grandma Rose was partly right. Not only is the fluid by itself good to strengthen Dr. Walker's hose (see previous discussion), but also the chicken fat in homemade soup has been shown to insert itself in bacterial cell walls and break them up: true penicillin-like activity. Now, Grandma's chicken soup remedy works only if you have that superinfection of a bacterial nature beyond the common viral cold (for which antibiotics are useless and should not be taken), but isn't it fine to know that Grandma didn't make that soup for us for nothing?

COLDS & FLU

When Should I Get a Flu Shot?

The "flu shot" is an inactivated vaccine (meaning it contains killed virus) that is given with a needle in the arm muscle. It is approved by the Food and Drug Administration for use in people older than 6 months, including healthy people and people with chronic medical conditions. Each shot contains three influenza viruses—one A (H3N2) virus, one A (H1N1) virus, and one B virus. The viruses in the vaccine change each year based on international surveillance and scientists' estimations about which types and strains of viruses will circulate in a given year. Approximately two weeks after vaccination, your body will have developed antibodies that provide protection against influenza virus infection.

If you are scheduling your flu shot around the time of a marathon or other race, getting the shot pre- or postevent is largely of no consequence. Because the viruses in the shot are killed (inactivated), you cannot get the flu from a flu shot. Almost all people who receive flu shots have no serious problems from them.

Some reported minor side effects that can occur are the following:

- Soreness, redness, or swelling where the shot was given
- Fever (low grade)
- Aches and pains

If these problems occur, they usually begin soon after receiving the shot and usually last only one to two days. So if you don't get the shot within 48 hours of your race, you should be fine.

In general, I believe anyone who wants to reduce his or her chances of getting the flu should get vaccinated; it is a personal choice if you are healthy. However, the Centers for Disease Control (CDC) advises that there are some folks who absolutely *should* get the shot:

- Children aged 6 months up to their 19th birthday
- Pregnant women
- People 50 years of age and older
- People of any age with certain chronic medical conditions
- People who live in nursing homes and other long-term care facilities

- People who live with or care for those at high risk for complications from flu, including health care workers, household contacts of persons at high risk for complications from the flu, and household contacts and out-of-home caregivers of children less than 6 months of age (these children are too young to be vaccinated)

There are some people who *should not* be vaccinated without first consulting a physician:

- People who have a severe allergy to chicken eggs
- People who have had a severe reaction to an influenza vaccination
- People who developed Guillain-Barré syndrome within six weeks of getting an influenza vaccine
- Children less than 6 months old (influenza vaccine is not approved for this age group)
- People who have a moderate to severe illness with a fever (they should wait until they recover to get vaccinated)

You can read more about flu shots at this CDC Web site: www.cdc .gov/vaccines/pubs/vis/downloads/vis-flu.pdf.

Don't forget eating healthily; getting your vitamins and minerals from healthy foods also helps build your immune system, as does your running!

Swine Flu

Ever since the swine flu pandemic in 2009, ER and family doctors have been telling me that they are seeing huge increases in patients seeking advice and reassurance that they don't have the swine flu. The swine flu is just one strain of influenza, and all the same issues about flu and vaccinations apply to the swine flu.

The initial symptoms of the swine flu virus are exactly like those of the regular flu: fever, muscle aches, sore throat, and runny nose with lots of mucus. There is more nausea, with diarrhea and vomiting, with this swine variety. Your primary care provider will probably take samples from your throat or your coughed-up mucus and send them to the state health laboratory for testing for confirmation that you have the swine flu. The good news is that this flu is killed by two antiviral medicines: Tamiflu (oseltamivir) and Relenza (zanamivir). Treatment seems to be most effective only if given within two days of the onset of symptoms.

Please do not panic! Most people recover quite well.

If you want more comprehensive information about the swine flu, see this page from the CDC: www.cdc.gov/h1n1flu/.

An Antibiotic to Avoid

Levofloxacin (Levaquin is the brand name for it) is an antibacterial antibiotic of the fluoroquinolone class of antibiotics. This class of antibiotics is used by physicians to treat some respiratory, lung, skin, and urinary infections. Within this class of drugs, Cipro has also been used to help in treating anthrax exposure.

The side effects of using fluoroquinolones have been well described in the literature, and in fact an FDA-mandated black box warning (a warning notice surrounded by a conspicuous black border on the package insert of a prescription drug) was put on Levaquin in July 2008. There is an increased risk of tendinitis, tendon tears, and tendon ruptures for up to six months after use of these drugs. The risk actually increases in transplant patients, those patients undergoing a course of corticosteroid treatment (as we sometimes use in sports medicine), and those over 60 (increase is dramatic for this group). There are lawyers out there just waiting to sue doctors who prescribe this medicine to athletes without giving them "informed consent," making sure they understand the risks involved.

As with all therapies, one must balance the good against the bad. If you were exposed to anthrax, it is deadly if inhaled. And Cipro is the atomic weapon against this horrible microbe; other antibiotics are not nearly as effective. So if exposed, personally, I would want the best chance at survival and would worry about a torn Achilles later. However, if the infection is not life-threatening and there are alternatives, I would be sure my doctor gave me one of the alternative remedies before turning to a fluoroquinolone!

Common Maladies
Ammonia-Smelling Sweat

A common question I hear at clinics, in my office, and on my Facebook page is, why does my sweat smell like ammonia? It is an important question and deserves a complete answer in this book.

Ammonia (the chemical term is NH_3) is a nitrogen breakdown product of amino acids in the body. Amino acids are the building blocks the body needs to make proteins. If your body is breaking down amino acids for energy (instead of using carbohydrate and/or fat), the nitrogen atom is chemically stripped off the amino acid molecule (which is then converted to glucose fuel); your body then processes the nitrogen in the kidneys and forms urea for excretion. If your kidneys cannot handle the load of urea, the nitrogen is excreted in your sweat as ammonia.

The best way to prevent the smell is to be sure you have enough carbohydrate fuel for your exercise. Runners who "eliminate" carbohydrates from their diet set themselves up for "ammonia sweat." A good preworkout meal usually does the trick. Also be sure to drink for thirst. Adequate fluid intake makes excretion easier.

So the next time you smell ammonia, don't worry that all your muscle protein is breaking down or that you are doomed to have smelly sweat forever. Look at what you eat before you exercise, add more carbohydrates and fat to your daily diet, and when you finish exercising, have some more carbohydrates and fat to replenish what you have used. Also make sure that you eat enough protein to help replace the amino acids used for energy. That should do the trick.

Athlete's Foot

Athlete's foot is the name given to a simple fungal infection (tinea pedis) that often occurs on the bottom of the foot or between the toes. The skin of the foot may be itchy, red, scaly, or peeling.

If you think you have athlete's foot, get an athlete's foot powder spray or cream at the local drugstore and use it twice daily for at least one week and up to four weeks (even if your symptoms subside) or for the length of time recommended on the package. Lamasil, Lotrimin, and Tinactin are common over-the-counter brands, and most drug-store chains have generic versions of these brands that work perfectly well. If the symptoms do not subside, see your doctor to make sure you are treating the right thing. If you are using a spray, apply it to the inside of your shoes as well.

In addition, keep your feet dry, and change your socks and shoes frequently—which, by the way, is the best way to avoid getting athlete's foot in the first place. If after each run, you always wash your feet, dry them thoroughly, and put on clean socks and a fresh pair of shoes, you will probably avoid athlete's foot altogether.

Athlete's Pseudoanemia

Hemoglobin, a molecule that carries oxygen, is found in red blood cells. The more oxygen our blood can deliver to our muscles, the better those muscles will work for us as athletes, so a shortage of hemoglobin, or a shortage of red blood cells, is especially bad news. The shortage is called anemia, and this term can also refer to a general reduction in overall blood volume.

The runners, triathletes, and swimmers who call me toward the end of their training season, having been warned after a preliminary blood screening that they show evidence of anemia, range from exasperated to frightened. A lot of longer competitions are held in the fall, and these people have been doing their endurance homework. Some have checked with their family doctor to make sure their chronic fatigue is just part of their hard training. Many have been told instead that they may need to be put on an iron supplement.

Now anemia can be a symptom of many different causes, from athletically induced microscopic internal bleeding (see page 67) to malignancies, and anyone who shows signs should follow a doctor's advice about ruling out the other possibilities. But what's really happening in most cases is what we call pseudoanemia. It happens all the time to athletes, and it's the body's healthy response to vigorous exercise. It has no symptoms; the only way you would know that you have it is when your doctor looks at your blood test and declares that you are "worn-out" or anemic!

Physicians use a value called hematocrit, the ratio of red cell volume to total blood volume, to look for signs of anemia. Normal values for adult men are 40 to 54 percent; for women, 37 to 47 percent. But working out can throw these values off. If you're not in great shape and you're just starting to exercise, dehydration shrinks your blood supply during a workout. But a well-conditioned body learns to expand its blood volume to handle the load.

Let's say a nonathlete with a normal blood volume and a hematocrit of about 45 percent starts working out. Sweating copiously, he loses blood volume, but the loss is all plasma. His red cell volume stays the same, so his hematocrit jumps to over 50 percent. Some weeks later, better trained and resting, both his red cell volume *and* his plasma volume will be up. But the body boosts the plasma more in order to decrease the blood's viscosity and make it a more efficient oxygen-carrying liquid. The result: a "crit" of perhaps 41 percent and, ironically, the possibility he'll be told something could be wrong.

Pseudoanemia is nothing to worry about and is totally benign: No supplementation or treatment is needed. It is, however, a diagnosis of "exclusion" in that you must be checked for and eliminate other causes before just letting this be. True anemia is nothing to fool with, and if there are possible causes, your physician will certainly need to rule them out. But if you're putting in the miles and are otherwise healthy, chances are any "anemia" you have is the pseudo kind, especially after a boosted summer training season.

Can I Run with a Hemorrhoid?

Be honest: If I told you not to run with this condition, how far would I get? You'd probably nod, smile, and then head out the door for another opinion. I can't get people to rest their stress fractures, never mind some swollen tissues in their backside.

Fortunately, I don't even have to try to tell you to do that. Running won't hurt you, but you should understand what's going on back there. Hemorrhoids are simply enlargements of the anal veins. They can originate inside or outside the anal opening, and internal ones can subsequently prolapse, or protrude outside. Either way, the

COMMON MALADIES

symptoms are the same: itching and/or pain that can be anything from mildly annoying to debilitating and possible bleeding. None of it calculated to exactly enhance an athlete's performance.

Athletics don't usually help. Lifting weights, for example, can drive an internal hemorrhoid outside, making it more likely to become thrombosed, or clogged with clotted blood. And running can simply irritate whatever problem you already have, increasing discomfort.

Step one, before running another step, is to have yourself checked by a physician. Don't be embarrassed; you'll be a lot better off if you get help. If the hemorrhoid is thrombosed, and especially if it's infected, you can be treated in the office with one or more simple surgical procedures. Take-home remedies, also highly effective, include sitz baths, stool softeners, and topical applications of creams, ointments, and suppositories.

Running won't do your hemorrhoids any good. But if you get them treated instead of just hoping they'll go away, they needn't remain a pain in the behind either.

Runner's Trots

Though so-called runner's trots has been sending athletes to the bathroom or the bushes for as long as anyone can remember, research has done little to identify exactly what causes it and, more helpfully, how it can be avoided.

The condition is stimulated by any intense endurance exercise and can strike people in the pool or on their bikes as easily as along the running route. Studies have shown that as many as 30 percent of the runners in a 10K race experience the symptoms: cramping, bloating, and loose bowel movements—sometimes accompanied by a little bit of blood.

The mechanism itself is controversial. One theory blames an enzyme the body produces while running that's known to increase peristalsis, or the food-pushing pulsing of the large intestine. Another suspect is so-called bowel ischemia, the process by which the body shunts blood to running legs and away from the digestive organs, causing them to reject what they can't digest.

Anxious about your race? Ironically that, too, could bring it on because stress can produce too few digestive stomach acids or—if prolonged—too many. Diet, allergies, and the mechanical jarring of the gut have all at one time or another been implicated.

But just because the medical community can't agree on what's happening to you doesn't mean that it has to happen. Here are a few proven strategies:

- The night before the race, eat a large, fiber-rich meal. Fiber speeds things up.
- Eat a generous meal about five hours before the race. If you can't, skip pre-race food completely.
- Always wait three to four hours after any meal to work out.
- The day of your race, reduce foods that provoke diarrhea: anything with caffeine or fiber, most dairy products, sugar substitutes (especially sorbitol), and vitamin C tablets.
- Cut back on gassy foods like apples, bananas, citrus fruits, beans, bran, carrots, cabbage, cucumbers, and raisins.
- Consider an antidiarrheal medication, but be warned: Some contain substances like phenobarbital, so you'd flunk any drug test. And they all dehydrate you, so they're not the best choice in long, hot-weather races.
- Some believe prostaglandins may mediate runner's trots. I have found that patients taking one NSAID (Advil, Motrin, Aleve, and ibuprofen are common anti-inflammatories) the night before a run alleviates the problem. A note of caution here: NSAIDs have been implicated as a strong risk factor for hyponatremia. Therefore, if you try this method as a last resort, be very careful not to overdrink; use thirst as a guide. We wouldn't want to cure the trots and give you a much more serious problem instead!

Short-distance athletes may be relatively safe; 10K or longer seems to be the running distance at which the problem usually kicks in.

As a physician, however, I just can't jump to the diagnosis of runner's trots without asking some very important questions first, which you in turn should also be asking your physician:

1. Is there any underlying condition causing these symptoms, such as colitis, gastritis, ulcers, or tumors? Some tests may be necessary to rule these out and will be determined by your history, family history, and physical examination.

2. Is this new to you, and has there been a recent history of travel? These same symptoms can be caused by infection or parasites and should be looked into.

3. Are there any food allergies involved? For example, does this always occur after you eat a specific type of food? If you change your diet, does the problem go away? A trip to an allergist might be necessary in this case.

If you answer "no" to all three of these questions, then feel comfortable that runner's trots it is, and try one of the strategies just outlined.

Side Stitch

Runners who pump their legs fast while breathing rapidly can get caught in the clenches of a side stitch. Although the medical literature and research reveal that the side stitch is not fully understood, most sports physicians agree that a side stitch is most likely a cramp in the diaphragm—the large muscle located between your lungs and abdomen that controls breathing. It's often caused when the diaphragm isn't getting enough blood during exercise.

Here's how a side stitch most likely happens. Pumping your legs increases the pressure on your abdominal muscles, which press up against the diaphragm. At the same time, rapid breathing expands your lungs, which presses down on the diaphragm. The dual pinching from above and below shuts off the flow of blood and oxygen to the diaphragm. Then the diaphragm cramps.

It's also been postulated that food may add to the diaphragm's distress. We know that a meal of less digestible food before exercising—fatty food, for example—makes the stomach heavier and increases the tugging on this diaphragm muscle.

Those new to endurance exercise, or those picking up exercise again after a layoff, seem to be most prone to side stitches. Beginners and untrained exercisers are more apt to take rapid, shallow breaths and may also push themselves before their abdominal muscles are ready to deal with the exertion. These muscles are not strong enough to protect against the bouncing that jostles internal organs and pulls on the diaphragm. Those with asthma also seem to get stitches due to the same type of rapid forceful breathing pulling on the diaphragm.

Prevention has been shown to be best accomplished by eating fewer fatty foods and eating further from the workout. Prestretching does not seem to help, nor does taking increased amounts of sodium, potassium, or magnesium supplements. With better endurance levels, the incidence of stitch will decrease.

For relief when you have a stitch, stop running, take long deep breaths, stretch to the sky, and then bend at the waist with your arms extended above your head. I call this the "swoosh" stretch because you look like the Nike logo.

As a doctor, I need to offer this word of caution: A side stitch can sometimes be felt all the way up to the shoulder. But this kind of pain *may* signal a heart attack, especially if it is on the left side and persists after you've spent a few minutes stretching. And if you get a side stitch each time you exercise, you could have a problem with blood flow to the intestine. So if you have these signals, see a doc! Otherwise, take comfort in the knowledge that as your training kicks in, these pesky side stitches will probably become less frequent and will eventually go away.

Treadmill Injuries

In my office practice, I see a huge increase in injuries in the fall and the spring, with the weather turning cold or warm and people therefore going from outside to treadmill and vice versa. These ailments are all soft tissue issues, involving ligaments, tendons, and muscles. As always, I go back to biomechanics to understand the reasons. When you run outside, your foot naturally out-toes. When you run on a treadmill, however, your foot travels parallel to the belt, negating the natural out-toe gait. This different gait is enough to stress soft tissues in a

COMMON MALADIES

way that is different from what they are used to, causing inflammation that lands you at the doctor's office, in pain and eventually in therapy to run pain-free again!

The solution also is quite simple. When transitioning from treadmill to outside or vice versa, cut back your workout by half and then increase it again gradually by 10 percent per week. I have found that when this simple cutback is done, the body readjusts without injury. Another solution is never to fully go cold turkey one way or the other. But treat each workout differently. Mileage or time inside is different and needs to be built up on a separate schedule from whatever you are doing on your outside runs. With this in mind, you should never have a transition problem again!

Triathlete Erectile Dysfunction

This is a common problem that I see in my patients who are new triathletes; I trust other sports docs do as well if they ask. In my experience, new triathletes develop this condition because they don't take seriously the importance of proper fit of a bicycle and seat. This is especially true when they borrow a tri bike from a friend and don't bother to reset the bike fit to suit their particular position. The aerodynamically favorable time trial bike position, employed by any bike with extended tri bars and a forward seat position, puts much more pressure on the rider's pudendal nerve than the standard road-racing position. My anatomy professor in med school called the pudendal nerve "the most glorious nerve in the male body." Glorious it is if it isn't pinched or bruised. The nerve is very superficial, lying just under a man's testicles, and an improper seat can hurt the nerve and hurt performance.

The good news is that if you get your bike fitted at the local bike shop, and perhaps change the seat to one of those gel seats, the condition resolves and you will be yourself once again! Being as compulsive about your bike as you are about your running shoes and training will pay great dividends, as longtime triathletes will tell you.

Chronic Problems and Cures
Exercise-Induced Asthma

Whether or not exercise-induced asthma (EIA) is a "silent epidemic of breathing problems among athletes," as it's dramatically been called, doctors now believe EIA affects many more active people than we once thought. It has been estimated that up to 15 percent of the general population may suffer from this easily overlooked and undiagnosed condition, and the incidence is probably not much lower among high-level athletes. Of the 597 members of the 1984 United States Olympic Team, 67, or over 11 percent, experienced symptoms of exercise-induced asthma. Whereas they had identified their condition and knew what to do about it, too many other athletes wrongly fault themselves for their breathing problems, assume they're just out of shape, and grow discouraged with their workouts. EIA may not be life-threatening, but it is uncomfortable and inconvenient, and it holds you back from doing your best. The good news is, EIA is manageable.

It's easy for an athlete to incorrectly assume that he or she is undertrained instead of simply experiencing a controllable breathing disorder because the symptoms of EIA are so similar to being out of shape: shortness of breath during or after exercise, chest tightness, coughing, and, of course, wheezing. And although EIA is only related to the better-known and more serious condition known as chronic asthma, what happens during an attack is similar. The bronchial tubes, which are the normally relaxed and clear pipelines into your lungs, get irritated and begin to constrict. The bronchial muscles around the tubes go into spasm—hence the term bronchospasm— even as a buildup of mucus in the tubes and the inflammation of the cells that line them clog up the airways even more. The alveoli (the little sacs where the air ends up) swell, too, suddenly unable to rid themselves of the air trapped inside. Your body can neither get in as much oxygen as it wants nor get out the stale air it no longer needs. No wonder you feel "out of shape."

Chronic asthma is generally caused by a persistent inflammation of the lungs' airways, a condition that can be triggered into a full-blown

CHRONIC PROBLEMS

and occasionally life-threatening attack by numerous environmental causes: pollen, cigarette smoke, airborne pollution, and, yes, exercise, as well as many other triggers. It generally requires daily treatment. Exercise-induced asthma, on the other hand, has one principal trigger: exercise. It generally requires only pre-exercise treatment. And though chronic asthma sufferers are also more likely to experience EIA, it doesn't work the other way around as far as we know.

You can't tell on your own whether your symptoms are exercise-induced asthma or just the normal experience of vigorous exercise with which it's so often confused. Only a doctor can make that diagnosis by testing you on equipment that can measure the amount of air you breathe in and out at rest, then during the beginning of an exercise session, and again several minutes into that session. That's because EIA does not strike immediately. It usually takes about 6 to 12 minutes of vigorous exercise to trigger an attack, and symptoms don't reach their peak until anywhere from 5 to 15 minutes *after* you've stopped your workout. Then, in somewhere from a half-hour to an hour and a half, they're gone completely.

Exactly what triggers an EIA attack is not yet completely known, but the consensus is that it starts with the sudden cooling of your body's airways. Exercise makes you breathe harder—usually suddenly—and your bronchial tubes must quickly warm and humidify a lot more air to get it ready for your lungs to tolerate. In the process the airways can cool down and dry out, and that cooling and drying can irritate sensitive tissues. So to protect themselves, the tissues contract into a state of bronchospasm.

That suggests a couple of possible strategies for managing the condition if it's not severe enough to warrant medication. Breathing through your nose to warm and moisten the air before it reaches the bronchial tubes is one common suggestion, though it's not very easy during anything but a mild workout. Wearing a face mask is probably more practical because it helps enrich inhaled air with heat and moisture from your skin. But just staying out of cold, dry air in the first place may be the best course. Use an indoor track or treadmill on crisp days, or consider a different workout that day. The warm, moist atmosphere of an indoor swimming pool is far less likely to set off an EIA episode than the cold air of an outdoor track. It's also known that in general, so-called high-ventilation sports that require continual exertion at a fairly high intensity, like long-distance running, cross-country skiing, and cycling, are more likely to bring on an EIA episode than "lower-ventilation," intermittent sports like golf, baseball, tennis, and weightlifting. And because EIA usually holds off for at least six minutes into your workout, the alternating work and rest periods of interval training keep some athletes symptom free.

What you *shouldn't* do is avoid exercise. Just the opposite, in fact. Aerobically fitter athletes don't breathe as heavily during their workouts, so even though their EIA might kick up at the same breathing rate, they're less likely to reach that rate in the first place. And no matter what your sport, if high concentrations of airborne irritants like pollen or pollutants increase your chance of an attack, it just makes good sense to exercise indoors on days when those pollutants are abundant.

Nature has created a convenient EIA loophole for some of us called the refractory period. That's the two to three hours after an exercise-induced asthma attack when the body for some reason is immune to another one or at least is much less likely to react as strongly. Warming up 45 minutes to an hour before the actual workout lets some athletes detour past the EIA episode and into the relatively symptom-free refractory zone.

Though some athletes can keep their EIA under control with simple workout strategies, most need the additional help of a medication. Bronchodilators, the first line of treatment, work to keep the airways relaxed and open and are used preventively (before exercise) or used during exercise to arrest an attack in progress. A relatively new class of drugs called leukotriene inhibitors block the chemical the body uses to constrict the bronchial muscles. The other main category is the anti-inflammatories, including inhaled corticosteroids, which reduce the hypersensitivity of asthma-prone airways. Most available medications are inhaled, though some are taken in pill form. No one medicine works best for everyone, and some athletes need a combination

CHRONIC PROBLEMS

Using an Inhaler and Determining How Much Medicine Is Left

Metered dose inhalers (MDIs) offer several advantages over oral EIA medications. Because the ingredients go directly into the lungs, they cause few side effects and take only minutes to work. But inhalers are not effective unless used correctly, and proper technique takes some mastering:

1. Remove cap and hold inhaler upright.
2. Shake inhaler.
3. Tilt your head back slightly and breathe out.
4. Open mouth with inhaler pointed at it, one to two inches away or with inhaler in mouth or using a so-called spacer to bridge the gap between the inhaler and your mouth.
5. Press down on the inhaler to release the medicine as you start to breathe in slowly.
6. Breathe in slowly for 3 to 5 seconds.
7. Hold your breath for 10 seconds to allow medicine to reach deeply into your lungs.
8. Repeat as prescribed. Wait 1 minute between puffs to permit second puff to go deep into lungs.

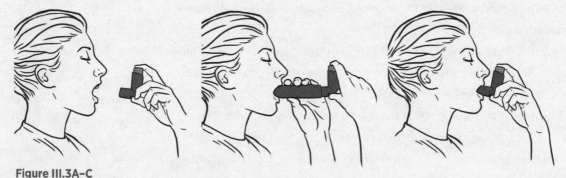

Figure III.3A–C

How to use an inhaler

To determine how much medicine is left, set your MDI's canister into a container of water and watch how it floats. The position will tell you how much medication is left inside.

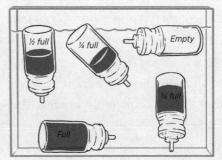

Figure III.4

Inhaler medication level

TABLE III.1   Medication for Exercise-Induced Asthma

Medication	Type*	Dose	How Long Before Exercise?	Lasts How Long?
Short-acting beta-agonists	B	2–4 inhaled puffs	15–30 min.	2 hr.
Salmeterol	B	2 inhaled puffs	30–60 min.	12 hr. (not to be taken more frequently)
Cromolyn sodium or nedocromil sodium	A	2–4 inhaled puffs	10–20 min.	2 hr.
Inhaled corticosteroids	A	8–16 inhaled puffs/day	(Ongoing therapy)	(Ongoing therapy)
Ipratropium bromide	B	2–4 inhaled puffs	1 hr.	2–3 hr.
Oral theophylline	B	Depends on condition and body weight	(Ongoing therapy)	(Ongoing therapy)
Leukotriene inhibitors	B	Depends on product	(Ongoing therapy)	(Ongoing therapy)

*A = anti-inflammatory; B = bronchodilator

for best control. Table III.1 lists the generic mainstays and indicates how they work and for how long. Side effects, in cases where they exist, are tremors, nausea, or heart palpitations.

Running and Diabetes

Type II diabetes (sometimes called adult-onset diabetes; it's where the body either doesn't produce enough insulin or becomes resistant to the effects of insulin) is common and usually runs in families. Historically, it has been well controlled with pills and diet. Control of blood sugar is also important in reducing the risks of kidney, eye, and vascular complications that can result from diabetes. Usually, adult-onset results improve with exercise and weight loss in overweight individuals.

Type II diabetics are now being given new-style basal insulin formulas that last for a long time; the two popular types, which differ slightly in makeup, are called Lantus and Levemir. The principal advantage of these types of basal insulins is that one injection from a graduated flex pen provides a steady-state release over 24 hours. An additional benefit is that they do not require multiple blood sugar tests during the day—although, while getting used to using them, you should measure those numbers during the day and report back to your doctor with a log. After a while, a morning test and an evening test are all you will need to do. And the injection is done with a small needle that you can barely feel.

CHRONIC PROBLEMS

Exercising with this new insulin is also easier. Once you establish your needs, you won't require a sugar test during your runs. Indeed, even though there are now testers as small as a pencil, I understand you may not want testing to interfere with your workout. The good news is that this insulin will help keep your sugars under control and not interfere with your training.

If you have Type I diabetes (sometimes called juvenile diabetes; it's a chronic condition where your pancreas produces little to no insulin), you have been controlling it with insulin from childhood, and so you are used to testing and adjusting your blood sugars. If you need to test your blood sugar during a race, you should be sure to bring your own testing equipment. You should also test the equipment and your blood sugar in your long training runs prior to the race so that you know what to expect. Insulin pumps make the process of maintaining proper blood sugar easier and are suitable for running. Ask your doctor about them.

Please remember that your training sessions are the time to practice what you will do on race day. Everyone has a different insulin requirement, and that is why it is so important for diabetics to monitor their blood sugar during training runs long before the event itself. And when you get to the race, do not rely on the event's medical team to test your sugar. Bring your own meter, and learn when you need to test yourself and how to eat. Remember, the goal is to make race day no different from a training run.

Deep Vein Thrombosis

Recently, at least five runners I know traveled across the country or to Europe by air and developed blood clots in their legs, a condition called deep vein thrombosis (DVT). According to their doctors, who were dumbfounded, these runners had no risk factors for a deep vein thrombosis: no birth control pills, no smoking, no past medical problems, no medications that they were taking regularly. Are runners more susceptible to this condition? More and more people are asking this question!

There is nothing written that I've read linking running and DVT, but given what I've observed, I do have some ideas. DVTs are blood clots that develop in the deep vein of the leg. This can be a very serious condition because the clot can break off, travel to the lung, and cause severe breathing difficulty and even death. Treatment includes hospitalization, anticlotting meds by IV, and then a regimen of anticlotting meds for months out of the hospital until the clot is totally dissolved.

Usually DVTs form after prolonged inactivity. Runners just may be the most active people we know, so initially it does not make sense that there would be an increased frequency among traveling runners. Physicians recognize such risk factors for DVTs as long flights of inactivity, bed rest after surgery, birth control pills, clotting disorders, cancer, smoking, heart disease, obesity, family history of DVT, and pregnancy. Symptoms of DVT are pain and swelling.

If you flex your foot upward and have calf pain, that is called a positive Homan's sign and indicative of a DVT. If in doubt, you should be checked by a physician immediately and get venous studies (an ultrasound, venogram, or pressure studies) to look for this serious problem.

The runners I mentioned earlier had none of the risk factors except the long flights, which one would think they could handle from their running. Could runners' bodies be more susceptible? I truly think it is possible. Runners' bodies adapt to running by making their leg vascular system more efficient: larger veins and arteries. So if you sit for a long time and are scrunched in an airplane seat, the blood can pool in your larger leg veins. That—coupled with the edge of the seat pushing on the back of your knee, preventing or slowing venous return—could be all you need to set up a clot.

What can you do to prevent a clot from forming? On flights of three hours or more, follow these guidelines:

- Do not sit in one position for more than an hour. Get up and walk up and down the aisle.
- Do calf stretches once an hour, standing and leaning against a bathroom wall.

- Stay well hydrated. As I always say, check your urine color: You want lemonade color, not clear and not amber like iced tea.
- Avoid crossing your legs at the knees and ankles.
- Wear graduated-compression stockings (the so-called TED stocking you can buy at your local pharmacy).
- If your doctor permits, take one baby aspirin four to six hours before your flight. It mildly prevents clotting as it does for heart patients.

If you follow this advice, you may prevent a clot in your well-adapted legs en route to your next race.

Arthritis

Does running cause arthritis? No, so please don't stop exercising if you've heard this old wives' tale! You'll be giving up all the benefits of aerobic exercise to avoid a condition we now know you're not bringing on yourself anyway. How do we know? The results from the legendary Framingham study, an intensive medical research project that followed its subjects for over 40 years, tells us so. Unlike previous studies, the Framingham study was longitudinal. It studied the same people over a long period, it studied both men (584) and women (820), and it studied everyone, not just runners.

Using an elaborate scale, researchers determined an "overall habitual physical activity level" for each subject, incorporating everything from heavy activities like running all the way down to sleeping. That way a 3-miles-a-day runner who sat at a desk the rest of the time would not necessarily be considered more active than a mail carrier who walked the whole town but might never run. Because this study was comprehensive, researchers believed it to be the best possible measure of repeated stress on the knees, making the conclusions highly reliable.

And when the numbers were crunched, the study reached a conclusion that was a beaut: "No association was shown between the level of physical activity during middle age and the occurrence of knee osteoarthritis in elderly persons." Street-talk translation: Today's exercise will not be paid for by tomorrow's pain.

Keep in mind two things, however. First, "no association" means no association. Today's exercise might not be *preventing* tomorrow's arthritis either. It has no apparent bearing on it either way. Second, the study did not follow subjects who exercised "excessively," which is to say at a level "far greater than that recommended to the public for health enhancement." The conclusions are for moderate exercisers only.

As for me, I finally have an answer for the aging athletes who come into my office every day, encouraged by the almost weekly research revelations that exercise is as close as we've ever gotten to a fountain of physical and mental youth. Plotting a training boost for increased fitness or for better race times, they still have a nagging question: "Doc, am I going to get arthritis from doing all this?" I always suspected they had nothing to worry about. Now I can tell them with full certainty to enjoy their training and racing.

The timing could not have been better. In addition to the familiar health rewards of exercise—lowered cholesterol levels, effective weight control, blood pressure benefits, not to mention a better sex life—there's been good news about exercise and the healthy heart. At least two separate studies have shown that the arteries of people who exercise regularly are a good deal more supple than those who don't. And though one study concentrated on marathoners, the other looked at runners who ranged from 54 to 75 years old and who averaged a relatively modest 30 miles per week. In both groups, the subjects' flexible arteries were more able to expand under stress. Because heart attacks are caused by that organ needing more blood than rigid-walled plumbing can deliver, the implications of the new findings are obvious and exciting. So every time you head out the door now, it's nice to know that your knees are ready to let you run to your heart's content and will be no worse for it.

Repeat Stress Fractures

Although women tend to have more stress fractures than men, when I see a patient in the office with recurring stress fractures, questions beyond gender need to be asked:

- Is there a biomechanical problem? Overpronation or leg-length discrepancy or both are common causes of overloading the bones in some way to cause stress fractures. A biomechanical evaluation by a sports physician is needed, and a custom orthotic may be necessary. You may need a more structured running shoe given the mileage you are doing.
- Are you strong and flexible enough for the workouts you are doing? A good strengthening and stretching program is also important to support your bones. If you are too tight or weak, too much stress may be stressing your bones.
- Are you increasing your mileage more than 10 percent per week? Increasing too fast may not allow your body to withstand the stress of a 40-mile-per-week regime.
- Is there a history of an eating disorder? It is very common, especially in women, that a disordered eating pattern in the past has led to weaker bones. A sports nutritional consult may be necessary to see if you are truly eating correctly and getting the food groups and vitamins and minerals necessary to stay healthy.
- Do you have osteoporosis? Bone density examination is very important for all with recurring stress fractures.
- Are your hormones off? In my mind, anyone who has three stress fractures within two years needs to see an endocrinologist. There are a number of hormones that can be looked at by an endocrinologist, especially pituitary hormones and estrogen and progesterone, which if off, can set the bones up to be more brittle.

Don't just assume a syndrome of recurring stress fractures is normal without asking these questions and getting answers. They just may save you from another!

Women's Health
Are Women More Suited for Endurance Than Men?

It sounds ludicrous now, but the running boom of the 1970s advanced quite a bit before women were even allowed to participate in many marathons. That's even more surprising in light of the latest scientific speculation about women's considerable endurance. Women, it now seems, might have been better equipped all along than men! At least that may be true as far as fuel is concerned when female endurance reserves are compared to those of the stronger men who were protecting the "weaker sex" as too delicate for such a grueling distance.

Whatever advantage women may possess probably doesn't kick in until a running event gets at least as long as the marathon—anything 26.2 miles or over, or its equivalent in another sport. And if our theories are correct, the longer the event is, the greater the possible advantage is.

Tracy Sundlun is a senior vice president of Competitor Group, which puts on the Rock 'n' Roll series of marathons and half-marathons, among other events, and he is also an Olympic track coach who has trained over 30 Olympic Trials Marathon qualifiers. In Sundlun's view, "The differences as you probe farther into the ultra-distances seem to indicate men and women are competing more on an even plane." Women are, indeed, beating men at ultradistances!

It may be a simple matter of fat stores—the increased body fat so many women athletes resent in themselves as some kind of dead-weight, wishing it were muscle instead. We know that after about 18 miles of steady running, the body begins to get low on glycogen—hitting the famous "wall"—and turns increasingly to other energy stores to keep going. But only recently, thanks in part to increasing numbers of women ultra-athletes and the times they're turning in, have we begun to suspect women may be more efficient at using that body fat early in a race and saving the glycogen for the long haul. A bigger tank and a more efficient fuel injection system? That could be.

Until now we've had only two major studies on the subject, and they conflict. But a recent one suggested that women may in fact have some way, not yet understood, of preferentially burning fatty acids better than men do. If that's the case, and we factor in that ability with women's greater body fat reserves, the implications are obvious. Assuming there is some glycogen sparing going on along the way, women might be able to get more out of that premium fuel than men do.

Larger fuel tanks aside, women ultra-athletes may also have additional chemical advantages that are not only perfectly legal but also perfectly natural. The more we find out about the powerful hormone estrogen, the more athlete-friendly it seems. For one thing, estrogen is a formidable antioxidant. And whatever your position on Dr. Kenneth H. Cooper's *Antioxidant Revolution*, a book that contends that exercise releases cancer-inducing free radicals and that ultra-athletes could be most at risk, it's highly probable that antioxidants help protect us from some pretty malignant conditions, whether we run over 60 miles a week (Cooper's "ultra" cutoff) or not. And though clean arteries don't help us run faster or longer, women athletes can be grateful that estrogen is also an antilipid agent, meaning it helps fight atherosclerosis, more commonly known as hardening and clogging of the arteries.

Even bottomless energy reserves wouldn't do much good for the athlete who is too pooped to access them, however. Muscles get tired as they run out of fuel, but the brain also has a mechanism by which it tells our body that we are weary. And if some recent studies are correct, estrogen attaches to a neurotransmitter in the brain, and the combination may delay the fatigue message. The result: The body doesn't feel as tired, so it doesn't *race* as tired.

Should all this prove true, does it mean women will ultimately own the longer distances? You'd be hard-pressed to find anyone who'd say so. "Do I believe that women marathoners will ultimately run as fast as men? I absolutely do not," declares Sundlun. But the fact that women are still relatively new to all this endurance work provides some pretty interesting headroom.

"Will women's marks continue to drop more precipitously than men's for a while? Absolutely," Sundlun adds. "And I think the evidence will prove that percentage-wise, the difference between the records in the ultra areas should ultimately be closer [between men and women] than at those events where power and muscle mass are more involved. It does look like women have some genetic qualities that would make them more efficient in those areas."

So, a word of warning to marathoning men: Even postmenopausal women have more estrogen than you do! Remember that the next time you're planning a really long workout and wonder whom to ask along to make you look good. Your female running friend may be slower, but she's probably a bundle of potential energy. When it's all over, you might be surprised to find that the "weaker sex" is you.

Menstrual Irregularities

The menstrual irregularities associated with running have long been recognized by doctors treating runners. Amenorrhea (absence of 3 to 12 consecutive menstrual periods) and oligomenorrhea (irregular, infrequent menstruation: 6 to 9 menstrual periods per year, or cycle length less than 90 days but greater than 35 days) have both been seen in exercising women in all sports. In fact, up to 50 percent of all women runners may see this happen to their periods.

Increased exercise causes a decrease in the hormones that control menstruation (for the technically minded, the hormones involved include gonadotropin-releasing hormone, or GnRH, from the hypothalamus; luteinizing hormone [LH] from the pituitary gland; and follicular stimulating hormone [FSH], also from the pituitary gland). Those hormones control your menstrual cycle, so a decrease in their levels or a change in their ratio means that your cycle goes out of whack.

The risk factors associated with these menstrual irregularities include the following:

- Increased mileage and intensity (different for everyone)
- Prepubertal training (regular training before puberty is reached)
- Delayed onset of initial period
- Low body weight/weight loss
- Low body fat/fat loss
- Nulliparity (never having carried a pregnancy)
- Never used oral contraceptive pills

- Diet deficient in protein and total calories
- History of a disordered eating pattern: bulimia or anorexia
- Family history of amenorrhea and/or oligomenorrhea
- Psychological stress

The more risk factors you have, the more likely you are to have irregular or absent periods.

The exact cause of the decreased GnRH, which in turn triggers the decrease of the other hormones, is still under discussion among physicians. Causes thought to be involved include b-endorphins and other hormones in the body whose levels are increased with exercise.

Evaluation and treatment of menstrual dysfunction are important because if left unchecked and brushed off as a normal consequence of running, this condition can lead to osteoporosis; stress fractures; increased growth of the endometrium (the mucous membrane lining the uterus), resulting in heavier, more painful periods later; and other soft tissue injuries.

A physician should take a thorough history and do a complete physical examination when you present with this problem. It is always necessary to check for pregnancy first even if you are using birth control; no system other than abstinence is foolproof. Your physician should evaluate your training schedule and any changes in it over the previous six months or the time you were having menstrual irregularity. A full diet evaluation should be done, too, as well as a review of what drugs you are taking and whether you have had recent stress fractures or psychological stress.

Next up is the laboratory evaluation. Your doctor will probably order these tests:

- Urine pregnancy test (if indicated).
- Thyroid stimulating hormone (TSH) and prolactin (luteotropic hormone, or LTH) levels (TSH is a hormone that helps regulate the thyroid gland; LTH is a hormone associated with lactation).
- A progestin challenge test (10 mg of Provera given for five days should bring on a period within two to five days, indicating adequate amounts of circulating estrogen in your body; this is considered a "positive test").

- FSH/LH levels if the progestin challenge test is negative. If the FSH/LH is high, ovarian failure, not a hormone problem, is the issue. If low, it is athletic amenorrhea.

Treatment is simple. Although decreasing training and increasing weight usually solves the problem, I know few runners who go for this plan. Instead, hormonal treatment to bring on periods every three months or use of oral contraceptives is an alternative that some ob-gyns feel comfortable prescribing. I have found that referral to a good sports nutritionist to be sure the protein intake is at 1–2 g/kg/day along with adequate calcium (1,500 mg/d) is a good first step. If stress is deemed the cause and running alone doesn't destress (or is causing the stress), a referral to a good psychologist sometimes does the trick.

Irregular Periods and Trying to Get Pregnant

Menstrual dysfunction (irregular or decreased periods) and ovulatory dysfunction (failure to ovulate) have been described in the medical literature among all female athletes. The incidence of these conditions in the sedentary population is 2 to 5 percent, whereas among female runners it is 10 to 50 percent. Risk factors include increasing mileage and intensity, low body weight, low body fat, and a diet deficient in protein and total calories. Some physicians believe psychological stress may play a role, but the literature is controversial in this regard. In my experience, quite frankly, I haven't seen the correlation. Regardless, these factors result in decreased hormonal regulation and control, thereby making it tougher for a woman to have normal periods and hence normal, easy conception.

Stopping running altogether will result in more psychological stress than anyone would be willing to tolerate and is not necessary. As I have said, if you are exercising, becoming a healthy mother and having a healthy baby result from continuing to exercise. But to conceive, the easy answer is usually to simply cut the mileage and intensity down by 50 percent until you conceive. If you are having trouble, it usually takes three to four months after you have cut down to make conception happen, but the good news is that in most cases this does the trick!

If this strategy does not work, the next important step is to see a local ob-gyn who specializes in endocrinology (a hormone/difficult pregnancy specialist). Be sure to ask:

- Are my hormone levels (FSH, LH, TSH, and Prolactin) normal?
- Am I pregnant and don't know it? This may sound stupid, but I have seen cases of pregnant patients who had a normal menses the first month and thought they weren't pregnant. It never hurts to repeat the test.
- Do I need a progestin challenge test? This is where you are given Provera (10 mg) orally for five days. Two to five days later, you should have a period. If this happens, then the test is said to be positive and indicative that your estrogen levels are low and need replacement or supplementation.
- Do I need a nutritional evaluation? Sometimes changing your eating habits may be all you need to do. A good sports nutritionist will go over a two-week meal diary and help you see if you are missing something.

I know that if you follow these steps, a new runner will likely be nine months away!

Running Doc's Pregnancy Physiology 101

Some people recommend stopping everything when pregnant; these are usually people without a firm knowledge of the topic. I actually wrote a chapter on this very subject in a medical textbook (R. Peter Welsh and Roy J. Shephard, eds., *Current Therapy in Sports Medicine 1985–1986* [Philadelphia: B. C. Decker, 1985], 122–125) while I was a medical student at Emory. The best way to understand what you can and cannot do while pregnant is to understand the physiology.

The physiological changes a woman's body goes through during pregnancy are very similar to those produced by strenuous exercise. Briefly, cardiac output (the volume of blood being pumped by the heart) increases by 30 to 50 percent over the nonpregnant resting state. The greatest cardiac output increase occurs during the first trimester when uterine blood flow is only slightly increased and before the placental vascular flow has begun. The maximal maternal blood volume is seen in the third trimester, giving the woman the ability to maximize cardiac output while working less.

Breathing rate (minute ventilation) during exercise also increases, especially in the third trimester. Because there is an increase in total body mass, additional oxygen is needed to perform any given activity.

Other normal physiological changes include a reduction of hematocrit (red blood cell volume) and a slight increase in hemoglobin concentration (hemoglobin is the oxygen-transporting protein in your blood). There are endocrine-based changes of carbohydrate and steroid metabolism. Curvature of the lumbar spine and relaxation of the cartilages of the symphysis pubis (the area in front of the pelvis) are normal changes.

In general, exercise brings about similar physiologic alterations. Changes are most pronounced for the cardiovascular and respiratory systems and less marked for the musculoskeletal and endocrine systems. If pregnancy and exercise are combined, there is a double physiologic impact. This very fact has led doctors, rightfully so, to recommend that if a prospective mother has not been involved in an exercise program prior to pregnancy, she should not be encouraged to begin one during her pregnancy!

If you are already a runner, however, you should absolutely *not* be discouraged from running. We now know, with our emphasis on physical fitness, that exercise is good not only for the general health of the nonpregnant female, but also for the health of the pregnant one. Exercise helps ensure an easier birth (in most cases) and a healthy fetus. Let's discuss this by trimester, each of which has unique recommendations, and postpartum:

First trimester. Avoid hot baths, whirlpools, and saunas, as high temperature has been linked to birth defects. This is not the time to begin an exercise program, but for those exercising, do not change your routine. Summer exercise should be conducted in the cool morning hours when there is light for outdoor activities but the temperature has not peaked; running after sunset when the temperature is cooler carries with it the increased risk of injury due to darkness. Do not overexert; now is not the time to try for a marathon PR. The greatest cause of heat stroke (and raised body temperature during running) is pushing one's self; take it easy, and hydrate appropriately. Finally, avoid medications, drugs, tobacco, and alcohol; take only necessary medications prescribed by a physician who knows you are pregnant.

Second trimester. All first-trimester recommendations continue. Also, now start strengthening muscles used in labor; time to begin your Kegel exercises (a series of muscle exercises designed by Dr. Arnold Kegel; ask your doctor about them if he or she hasn't already gone over them with you) to improve the muscle tone of your pelvic floor. Augment your diet with iron and calcium supplements as the developing fetus begins to demand these elements in increasing amounts. A good physical examination by an ob-gyn at this time is critical to determine the competency of the cervix (the mouth of the uterus, which helps hold the baby inside). A "weak" cervix is the most common contraindication for running from now until the baby is born. Don't run after this exam without your practitioner's OK.

Third trimester. Although research has shown that continued running during third-trimester pregnancy is not harmful to the developing child, avoid exercises that may compromise fetal blood flow, particularly venous return—standing in place for long periods of time or lifting heavy weights, for example, are bad ideas. Besides running, ideal exercises include yoga, walking, and swimming (until near term but certainly not after rupture of the membranes).

Postpartum. So now the baby has been born. What next? Depending on the type (and "normality") of delivery, you should resume an exercise program as soon as you and your attending physician or nurse-midwife feel comfortable. Even while still in the hospital, you can begin to restore muscular tone to your abdomen and pelvis. This helps prevent urinary incontinence and uterine prolapse and enhances a return to normal sexual activity. Exercise also promotes blood flow, avoiding such complications as varicose veins, leg cramps, edema, and blood clot formation. Improved circulation promotes healing of traumatized pelvic tissues and strengthens uterine and pelvic ligaments and tendons. Kegel exercises to strengthen the pelvic floor are recommended.

As an added benefit, exercise in the postpartum period has been shown to decrease the incidence of postpartum depression. We all know how we feel if we don't exercise, so get those endorphins kicking!

The major exercises to *avoid* postpartum are those that employ a knee-chest position (doing squats, lying on your back and bringing your knees up, facing down on bent knees, and doing similar routines). There have been reported complications (neurological and vascular) with these positions, so stay away from these until your physician says it's OK to do them.

PART IV
INJURY MANUAL 101

Injury Manual 101

FEET AND ANKLES

Black Toenails

> QUICK GUIDE: BLACK TOENAILS
>
> **Symptoms:** Pain, black toenails.
>
> **How it occurred:** Repetitive trauma of the toe or toenail hitting end of shoe.
>
> **What the doctor may do:** If painful, put a hole in the toenail to release pressure.
>
> **Likely treatment:** Prevention is key. Leave one thumbnail's distance between longest toe and end of shoe. Trim toenails.

Bleeding that occurs under a toenail is from repetitive trauma where that toe hit the end of your shoe. If the toenail has leaked to relieve the pressure that can cause pain, so much the better. If it hasn't and the condition is painful, a doctor can put a hole in the nail to relieve the pressure. In any case, the black color is just the blood under the nail drying up. It will be reabsorbed. The nail may die and fall off; no worries, a new nail will grow in behind it.

To prevent black toenails, follow these guidelines:

- Make sure your running shoes fit properly. Buy them at the end of the day when your feet are most swollen. Make sure there is a thumbnail's distance between your longest toe (which may be your second toe) and the end of the shoe.
- Make sure your toenails are trimmed before you run. Sometimes an extralong nail can hit the front of the shoe and cause bleeding beneath the nail.

- Make sure your insole or orthotic is not slippery. Sometimes slippery insoles make the foot slide forward and the toe hits the front. Try putting a nonslippery covering over your insole or orthotic; something like those Dr. Scholl's foam pads (white with little holes in them) you can find in almost all drugstores will work for this purpose.

Achilles Tendinitis/Tendinosis

QUICK GUIDE: ACHILLES TENDINITIS/TENDINOSIS

Symptoms: Pain and swelling at Achilles tendon.

How it occurred: Repetitive overuse due to biomechanical problem, either overpronating or supinating. Also can be due to overly tight calf muscles.

What the doctor may do: Palpate tendon, dorsiflect foot to evaluate calf tightness. Order MRI or ultrasound to evaluate tendon. Doctor should also check your running form and wear pattern on your running shoes.

Likely treatment: Calf stretches. Gait analysis. Orthotics or orthotic adjustment. PRP injection. Physical therapy. Electronic stimulation. Ultrasound. Time back to running will depend on severity of injury.

NOTE: Cortisone injection should be avoided because it will weaken the tendon.

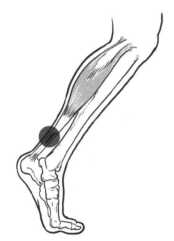

Figure IV.1A

Achilles tendinitis, side view

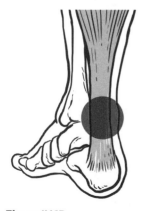

Figure IV.1B

Achilles tendinitis, rear view

Any sport that keeps you on your feet and uses a pushing-off motion can produce Achilles tendon trouble. Orthotics (see page 68) are usually prescribed, but stretching is always your first defense.

The Achilles tendon, which is formed from your calf muscles, can be pushed beyond its limits and become inflamed. That's the tendinitis to which most athletes ascribe pain. There can also be some swelling tendinosis, or chronic tendinitis, above the upper heel. But every time the tendon gets inflamed, and certainly every time the pain comes from more serious microtears in the overused tissue that can easily be mistaken for tendinitis, the Achilles grows just a little weaker.

What brings the condition on besides simple overuse? The Achilles is vulnerable to misuse. Designed to do its job of guiding the heel in a vertical plane, it's intolerant of the rolling of the ankle when it overpronates (rolls inward) or supinates (rolls outward).

Stretching and an orthotic can help prevent the inflammation by biomechanically allowing the tendon to pull in proper alignment.

But a calf muscle routinely loosened by conscientious stretching every day and after a workout cuts the tendon some slack, particularly in stiffer athletes, reducing the tendon's role as a shock absorber—for which it's not very well suited anyway. So on those hectic days when stretching seems too much of a bother, remind yourself that a neglected and partially torn tendon needs to rest and heal in a cast for six to eight weeks unless you like courting a rupture.

And if that tendon *does* pop? The gulf between the two ends creates a hole you can actually feel. A clock has just started ticking, during which the tendon's two ends will drift apart. As soon as possible you must decide if you want the rupture repaired by surgical reattachment of the ends—the best choice for most athletes. After the operation, you will have to wear a cast or cast boot at first and then undergo probably 9 to 12 months of therapy. The sooner the surgery's done, the easier the repair. Or you can just go into a cast for maybe 8 to 12 weeks and accept whatever healing nature is able to provide—probably a weaker result and longer recovery.

Given all this, a couple of minutes of prevention doesn't seem like such a bother after all. Do both the gastroc (upper calf muscle) stretch and the soleus (lower calf muscle) stretch whenever you're near a wall and have the time. As for the Achilles tendon stretch, once a day for a minute should do it. For both, the more, the better.

Heel lifts alone (orthotic inserts that go only under the heel; see page 69) are a big NO. They shorten the muscle tendon complex. Yes, you "feel" better wearing them, but next time out running, when you stride a little farther or speed up, that shortened complex will now tear. That, you don't want or need! So, please stay away from those heel lifts.

So what do you do if stretching alone doesn't work? The longer you take before you seek help, the longer the problem will take to fix. All structures in the body constantly remodel (at different rates). The Achilles tendon gets its strength by its fibers lining up in parallel. If its originating calf muscles are inflexible, living in an environment of overpronation and inflammation (tendinitis), remodeling proceeds

Three Stretches for Your Achilles

Figure IV.2

Gastroc stretch

Lean into wall, keeping affected leg back straight, heel on floor and foot turned slightly outward. Stretch should be felt in upper calf.

Figure IV.3

Soleus stretch

Similar to gastroc stretch with affected leg back but knees slightly bent; lean into wall until stretch is felt in lower calf.

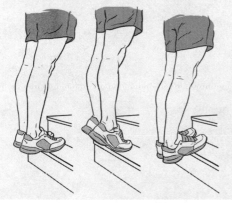

Figure IV.4

Achilles tendon stretch

Stand with toes on stair, heels off the edge. Rise up on toes, then down as far as possible. Return to starting position.

with the fibers lining up every which way instead of parallel. This results in a weakened, swollen, painful tendon, which is the definition of tendinosis (instead of tendinitis). This tendon is more easily prone to tear, and you will need a full-length flexible orthotic (worn full-time instead of just when running) and physical therapy for eight or more weeks minimum. The therapist is specifically trained to bring blood flow into that tendon without breaking it. In this case, PRP injections (see sidebar on page 124) can greatly speed the healing and do not weaken the tendon like cortisone may.

If you have developed tendinosis, I know your next question is, can I run? You can run in that flexible full-length orthotic if you can maintain your running form. This may require slowing down and shortening stride length. Realize that your sports doctor should clear you before you return to speed, and when you do, I suggest getting with a good coach and progressing gradually back to your old speed. Don't rush, or you will only hurt something else!

Retrocalcaneal Bursitis

QUICK GUIDE: RETROCALCANEAL BURSITIS
Symptoms: Pain at Achilles tendon.
How it occurred: Chronic inflammation of bursa due to overpronation or supination and friction.
What the doctor may do: Palpate. Dorsiflex foot to check flexibility of calf muscles. Gait analysis. MRI or ultrasound.
Likely treatment: Calf stretching. Orthotic or orthotic adjustment. Cortisone injection in the bursa, *not in the tendon*. PRP injection. Physical therapy. Electronic stimulation. Surgery is last resort (and rarely required).

I get a lot of questions about problems in the Achilles area that don't respond to traditional treatment. However, retrocalcaneal bursitis is a commonly missed diagnosis that mimics Achilles tendinitis.

Immediately in front of the Achilles tendon's insertion into the heel bone is a bursa, or fluid-filled sac, whose primary purpose is to permit smooth gliding of the tendon over the bone. This bursa can become inflamed due to either excessive pronation (inward roll of the foot) that is not properly controlled by an orthotic or friction caused by the heel

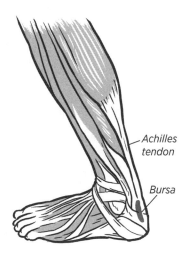

Achilles tendon

Bursa

Figure IV.5
Retrocalcaneal bursitis

Platelet-Rich Plasma (PRP) Injections

Platelet-rich plasma (PRP) injections are for real! I consider them as major an advance in sports medicine as the MRI. They are now widely available, and I am doing them in my office as a treatment to speed healing and quickly get runners back to running.

Here is how PRP works: A physician takes a sample of your blood (approximately 20 cc), spins it down for 14 minutes with a special centrifuge (this separates out a layer of platelet-rich plasma), and then injects the PRP into the area of a muscle tear, tendinitis, tendinosis, ligament sprain or inflammation, torn meniscus, inflamed patella, or inflamed fascia. The injection of the patient's own platelet-rich plasma accelerates healing so fast it is truly remarkable. For example, the Pittsburgh Steelers' Hines Ward had this done in the two weeks before the 2009 Super Bowl to resolve a sprained medial collateral ligament and did great. I have seen patients do just as well, though sometimes it takes two or three injections.

PRP works naturally and we all like that. The process is based on the same principle as when you get a laceration: Platelets come in to coagulate the area but also send out signals for the body to bring in multiple healing factors. In the case of PRP, the healing factors come in with the injection. Putting PRP at an injury site multiplies the body's healing response by a factor of seven or higher!

The upside of this treatment is huge: It is all natural, it can be done in a doctor's office, it speeds healing, and it doesn't weaken structures as cortisone shots can do. The only downside is expense: One injection can be costly, and most insurance plans do not cover this treatment or only cover it partially. More and more doctors are performing this procedure around the country, however, and we all hope in the future that insurance companies will cover this treatment that works so well.

of a constrictive running shoe. The resulting pain is very similar to that of Achilles tendinitis. This condition tends to fool physicians unfamiliar with treating runners, but the diagnosis is simple for those who know what to look for and requires no expensive testing.

Treatment for this condition is fairly straightforward. Proper-fitting shoes and full-length, flexible orthotics are essential as a first step. Next, physicians often recommend physical therapy, stretching, and anti-inflammatories. Tough cases that go on for six months or longer usually need stronger anti-inflammatories, longer therapy, and sometimes an injection of depomedrol or PRP (see page 124). Be careful, however; a doctor who is unfamiliar with the condition may inject the tendon and not the bursa. I have seen one case that did not respond to any of these treatments and required surgery to cut away the inflamed bursa.

Luckily, such measures are rarely necessary. If you have the problem and take care of it early, you should soon be running pain-free.

Plantar Fasciitis

QUICK GUIDE: PLANTAR FASCIITIS

Symptoms: Painful arch, most painful in morning when you get out of bed.
How it occurred: Tight arch connective tissue, tight calves, overpronation or supination, bone spur from calcaneal bone toward arch.
What the doctor may do: Palpate. X-ray to look for bone spur. Gait analysis. MRI to look for tear of arch connective tissue (plantar fascia). Check calf flexibility.
Likely treatment: Calf stretches. Arch support orthotics or orthotic adjustment to take pressure off plantar fascia. Physical therapy. Golf ball exercise (see text). PRP injection.

NOTE: Do not have a cortisone injection; it will weaken plantar fascia and may cause a tear.

Tight arches, overpronation, and tight calves all lead to inflammation of the connective tissue that forms this arch of your foot. This condition, plantar fasciitis, can be very painful, from your first step in the morning.

Fortunately, treatment is easier than most. Good arch supports or orthotics are key. Stretches of the calf relieve arch tightness as the heel bone acts like a fulcrum pulling back the arch tissues if too tight. Perform the gastroc and soleus stretches regularly (see page 122)—you can't do them too much.

Finally, the magic cure is to roll a golf ball under the arch for a half-hour once a day. (I know; a half-hour is a long time to perform one exercise, but that's what it takes. Once you master this exercise, it is easy to do while you work at your desk.) This may hurt the first week. Keep going because by week two the pain will be gone!

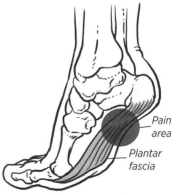

Pain area

Plantar fascia

Figure IV.6

Plantar fasciitis

Heel Bursitis, or "Faux Fasciitis"

QUICK GUIDE: HEEL BURSITIS

Symptoms: Pain in middle of heel, which mimics plantar fasciitis, except pain is rarely felt first thing in the morning with the first step.

How it occurred: Friction, age (fat pad in heel atrophies with age, causing more friction with each step).

What the doctor may do: Palpate. Gait analysis. Examine running shoes for sufficient cushion. Thorough physical exam should confirm diagnosis; further testing rarely needed.

Likely treatment: Cushioned footwear. Orthotic or orthotic adjustment if needed. Calf stretches. Cortisone or PRP injection.

Ever hear of "faux fasciitis"? Probably not. I made up the term because I needed some way of describing this deceptive foot arch pain that discouraged runners call me about as they increase their mileage when the weather gets better in spring. The typical story is that the runner wakes up one morning, takes a few steps out of bed, and is suddenly beset with heel pain while walking. The ailment is diagnosed as plantar fasciitis. After a visit to the doctor, the athlete dutifully does everything prescribed (stretches, orthotics) and yet does not get better.

Aging heels and flimsy footwear can produce symptoms that are deceptively similar to plantar fasciitis. But if you are lucky, the problem is really due to what I call faux fasciitis, better known as heel bursitis: an inflammation of a tiny liquid-filled sac on the bottom of the heel bone. It is as easy to treat as it is painful, but you need to understand how it got there in the first place to keep it from coming back.

Aging heels usually start the process. Though most of us would love to lose fat automatically as we get older, the heel is one of those places it actually happens. And that's a shame because it's one of the places where we can least spare the loss. Nature's own shock absorbers, these fat pillows protecting the heel bone thin out with age, while whatever padding is left gets squeezed to the outside of the heel by the constant pounding of long jumping, hurdling, or running. The heel becomes useless for protecting the bone beneath, which

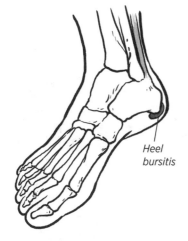

Heel bursitis

Figure IV.7

Heel bursitis, or "faux fasciitis"

can now become painfully bruised or, far worse, develop a fracture from the stress. Long recoveries, both.

But chances are good that what's actually happened is neither a bruise nor a fracture but a third possibility: an irritation of the bursa. It is supposed to cushion and lubricate the area, not swell in irritation and hurt severely while buried in the flesh of the back part of your foot. But the bursa will take only so much pounding, especially the kind that high-mileage athletes in supple, thin, minimally cushioned "road feel" shoes or wearers of hard leather full-length orthotics dish out to their heel bones.

An inflamed bursa is like butter boiling in a pan: Turn the heat up and it splatters. What is really needed is ice (no heat) and anti-inflammatories to treat the initial symptoms and inflammation. A cortisone local injection is needed 50 percent of the time if the symptoms don't abate with the first treatment alone. PRP (see page 124) is a last-resort option. Then a look at prevention is key: better padded shoes and a flexible, not hard, orthotic (possibly with a central cutout to give extra heel padding). Calf stretches to relieve a tensed foot fascia around the bursa also help considerably. Do the gastroc and soleus stretches regularly (see page 122).

Pump Bump

> QUICK GUIDE: PUMP BUMP
> **Symptoms:** Painful bump in back of heel.
> **How it occurred:** Friction from ill-fitting shoe at heel cup.
> **What the doctor may do:** Physical exam, both with and without shoes. Palpate area.
> **Likely treatment:** Better fitting shoes. Cortisone injection. If symptoms do not resolve, PRP injection.

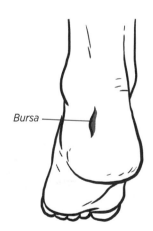

Bursa —

Figure IV.8

Pump bump

Sometimes a "bump" forms on the outside of the heel after a runner wears running shoes that do not fit snugly around the heel. Constant rubbing can cause a fluid-filled sac (bursa) to form. Overpronation can speed this process. This bursa can become irritated and painful.

Prevention is the key. There is nothing better than properly fitted shoes; make sure they don't slip while you are running. If you need orthotics to correct overpronation, please get them. And if the irritation doesn't die down or is unbearably painful, either an anti-inflammatory gel (like Voltarin gel) or a cortisone shot will help.

Calcaneal Stress Fracture

QUICK GUIDE: CALCANEAL STRESS FRACTURE

Symptoms: Pain in heel bone.

How it occurred: Chronic overuse injury. Overpronation, shoes without sufficient cushion.

What the doctor may do: Physical exam. Gait analysis. MRI useful to differentiate stage of injury (stress syndrome versus stress fracture). Bone density test to rule out osteoporosis or osteopenia.

Likely treatment: Orthotic with central cutout in heel to relieve pressure on bone. Cushioned shoe. Exogen bone stimulation. Calf stretching. No weight-bearing exercise for 6 to 8 weeks. PRP around bone—not in bone—on both sides of calcaneus shows promise as treatment.

NOTE: Cortisone injection is not indicated.

Calcaneal stress fractures are quite common as we age, sorry to say. The calcaneus is the bone that forms the heel of your foot, and it can be fractured through repetitive stress. The fat pad under the heel is supposed to protect this area, but it happens to be the only fat in the body that actually atrophies as we age, thereby setting up heel bruises, heel bursitis, and calcaneal stress fracture.

Even if overpronators wear proper shoes, they can, through repetitive stress, bruise the calcaneal bone until a stress fracture results. I look at a stress fracture as something similar to a cracked eggshell on a hard-boiled egg. The difference is that the stress fracture can be cured, but be aware that the only way to get this to heal is to be off it from six to eight weeks! I know this is tough. But even walking on it blows on a burning ember, so to speak, and will never allow it to heal. Sometimes a bone stimulator may speed the process (ask your doctor).

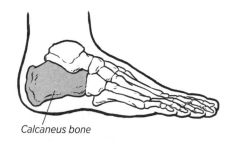

Calcaneus bone

Figure IV.9

Calcaneus bone (heel bone)

If you have been wearing racing flats for long training, you need to ditch them and get shoes with more padding. You will need the stability and cushion in a more structured shoe, and there is a good chance that you will need orthotics. If you don't make those changes, this injury will recur. If calcaneal stress fractures become a recurring problem, I would routinely also check your bone density to be sure you are not osteopenic (you have low bone mineral density) or osteoporotic (you have osteoporosis, or decreased bone density). Sad to say, decreased bone density is one of the joys of old age, but your doctor can help you counter many of its symptoms with medication—mainly vitamins— and some prescribed exercises.

Cuboid Syndrome

QUICK GUIDE: CUBOID SYNDROME
Symptoms: Pain in arch, which mimics plantar fasciitis, but pain not usually seen with first step in the morning.
How it occurred: Repetitive inversion.
What the doctor may do: Physical exam. Palpation. Manipulation during physical exam should show relief of pain. Gait analysis.
Likely treatment: Cuboid pad and no running for 6 weeks. Repeat manipulation of bone back into place weekly. Orthotic or orthotic adjustment. PRP speeds healing of the ligament.

Cuboid syndrome is a subluxation (partial dislocation) of the cuboid bone in the foot. The cuboid bone essentially moves out of place due to ligaments weakened from repetitive inversion (the foot repeatedly turning inward while running). The pain goes right up under the arch of the foot. It mimics plantar fasciitis but doesn't go away with standard treatments. X-rays and MRI are usually not useful because they are normal. An examination with tenderness on this bone makes the diagnosis. Treatment is conservative, normally involving manipulation and then strapping with tape and/or employing an orthotic with a cuboid pad to hold the bone in place as the ligaments heal (see the accompanying illustration). Maximum downtime is six weeks; if

Figure IV.10

Cuboid syndrome

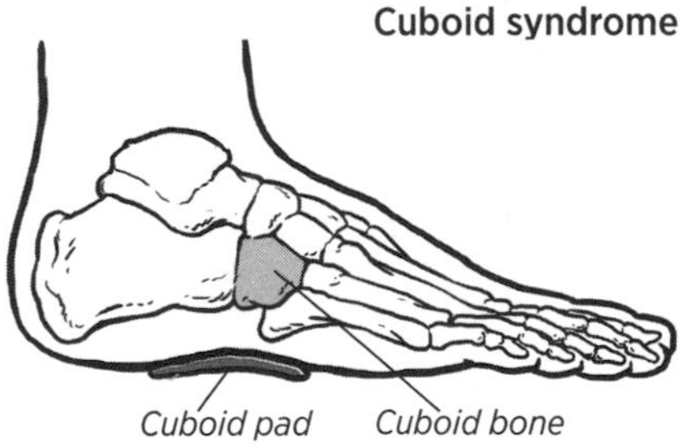

Cuboid pad   Cuboid bone

a runner is in a hurry, I have seen PRP (see sidebar on page 124 for further information) injected into the ligaments to speed healing while the runner wears the strap or orthotic.

Eli Manning, the football quarterback, was reported to have something different in 2009. News outlets reported that he had a "stress syndrome" of his cuboid bone. Again, the bone becomes stressed from repetitive inversion, and the condition, if not corrected, will lead to a stress fracture. The pain is exactly the same as that of plantar fasciitis, but there is usually less or no pain with palpation of the bone. This is not ligamentous and is easily seen on an MRI. Rest, an orthotic to protect from more inversion, and a bone stimulator are useful in reversing this and preventing a stress fracture. Recovery time varies with the severity, and all bets are off for a quick fix if the syndrome becomes a stress fracture.

Hallux Valgus (Bunion)

QUICK GUIDE: HALLUX VALGUS

Symptoms: Pain at a bulging deformity at great toe.

How it occurred: Heredity, chronic overpronation.

What the doctor may do: Palpate area to judge pain. Gait analysis. Measure toe angle using a standing X-ray. MRI to look for inflammation or stress fracture.

Likely treatment: Orthotics or orthotic adjustment to slow progression. Toe separators to slow progression. Cortisone injection to reduce inflammation. Recovery time and treatment depend on severity and pain level. Surgery may be required, with up to 6 months' recovery time.

NOTE: PRP is not useful.

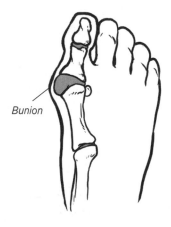

Bunion

Figure IV.11

Hallux valgus (bunion)

Bunions are always a problem for athletes, especially for runners. The medical term for this condition, hallux valgus, describes a bony, large bump that forms on the inside portion of the great toe's first joint. The great toe angles in a deformed way toward the other toes laterally. This bump may swell, becoming red and sore, and the skin will probably thicken at the great toe base.

The cause of this deformity is twofold. First, as I always say, "you can't pick your parents." If you look at your parents' feet, they probably have the same problem; it definitely is inherited. In addition, forefoot overpronation magnifies this deformity with every step so that runners inadequately controlled with full-length orthotics and/or those with tight-toed shoes and high heels exaggerate the deformity and accelerate the progression.

Understanding the progression can help slow it down but not eliminate it. Be sure to have a flexible full-length orthotic when you run. Wear looser-fitting shoes around the toes, and avoid high heels on a regular basis. You can also try toe separators—not the thick silicone ones that are very common but the thin foam or silicone ones.

If none of this works, anti-inflammatories and corrective devices may be used to push the toe into place in a better position. These devices rarely work, however, and if you get to this point, surgery is probably in your future.

Some surgeons cosmetically grind the bump down; avoid that approach, as the problems afterward usually are greater than the bunion itself. If you need surgery, opt for the "real" one, in which the toe is straightened through the removal of a piece of bone. That is the far better way to go, despite the long (up to six months) recovery time.

I'm sorry there is no great answer for a deformed toe that can only get worse. If you have this, I do feel your pain. Try the steps outlined here to slow it down so that you don't come to surgery.

Jones Fracture: Fifth Metatarsal

QUICK GUIDE: JONES FRACTURE

Symptoms: Pain along outer side of foot on the bone (fifth metatarsal).
How it occurred: Overpronator slamming outside of foot on ground over time. Not enough correction by orthotic. Not enough cushion in shoe.
What the doctor may do: Palpate area. Gait analysis. X-ray. If X-ray is negative, MRI to look for stress syndrome or stress fracture.
Likely treatment: Orthotic or orthotic adjustment with extra cushion on outer side. Cushioned shoes. Exogen bone stimulation. No running for 6 to 8 weeks. If bone is broken all the way through, surgery will probably be necessary to insert a screw.

NOTE: PRP shows promise in healing stress fractures faster.

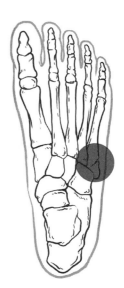

Figure IV.12

Jones fracture

Sometimes, overpronators land very hard on the outside of their foot before rolling inward. They are what I call "forefoot floppers." Don't try to look that up because it is my own term for this heavy landing that puts strain and stress on the fifth metatarsal bone (the bone behind your small toe bone). That is why, when I make orthotics, I watch my runner run on a treadmill or down the hall barefoot to see exactly how he or she needs to be controlled. In this type of case, a lateral piece of material is placed on the orthotic to cushion and redirect the landing to take stress off that bone.

Fractures that result from stress usually end up in the proximal end of the fifth metatarsal: the Jones fracture (first described in 1902 by a Welsh orthopedic surgeon, Sir Robert Jones, who sustained this injury while dancing). Because blood flow is irregular in this area, the bones sometimes need a screw placed in surgery to allow them to heal properly. Without the operation, you risk a "nonunion" and further surgeries and layoffs beyond the surgery now recommended. Do not hesitate on this one—take your doctor's advice if he or she recommends this surgery. You want a long running career; this will be only a blip in it!

If you feel discomfort in training, you may be stressing the bone. Instead of ignoring the discomfort, see a sports doc; it could easily be prevented by a simple adjustment of your orthotic.

Metatarsal Stress Fracture

QUICK GUIDE: METATARSAL STRESS FRACTURE
Symptoms: Pain over metatarsal.
How it occurred: Chronic overpronation or supination.
What the doctor may do: Palpate area. Gait analysis. X-ray. MRI.
Likely treatment: Orthotic or orthotic adjustment. Cushioned shoe. Exogen bone stimulation. No weight-bearing exercise for 8 to 12 weeks.

NOTE: PRP shows promise in speeding healing.

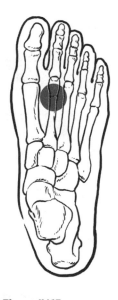

Figure IV.13

Metatarsal stress fracture

Overpronation can cause stress of the other metatarsal bones (the *Jones fracture* described previously affects only the fifth metatarsal). Early recognition of discomfort and subsequent adjustment of an orthotic by a sports doc can prevent a full-blown metatarsal stress fracture and an 8- to 12-week layoff. Water running therapy (jogging in water deep enough that your feet don't touch the bottom, also called "aqua therapy") during the healing process is not as fun as being on the roads, so early attention to any metatarsal distress is a very good idea.

If you do get a stress fracture, all weight-bearing exercise—including cycling—must cease! You may be given an Exogen bone stimulator, which when worn daily may speed healing. You won't feel the current from the bone stimulator, but in certain cases it can accelerate the healing process considerably.

Foot Tendinitis

QUICK GUIDE: FOOT TENDINITIS
Symptoms: Pain with movement.
How it occurred: Chronic overpronation or supination.
What the doctor may do: Palpate area, and have you move your foot against resistance of his or her hand to mimic pain. Gait analysis. X-ray or MRI usually not needed for diagnosis.
Likely treatment: Orthotic or orthotic adjustment. Ice massage. Physical therapy. Electronic stimulation. Cortisone injection around tendon *but not in it*. PRP for faster result.

As a general term, foot tendinitis covers peroneal tendinitis, anterior tibialis tendinitis, and posterior tibial tendinitis. The unifying theme is tendon trouble somewhere in the foot. Tendons attach muscles to bone and with their contraction cause movement. All of these muscle tendon units have muscles in the lower leg and extend their tendons across the ankle. The tendons then insert into foot bones to make movement. Overpronation or supination may cause the tendons to rub and become inflamed (tendinitis).

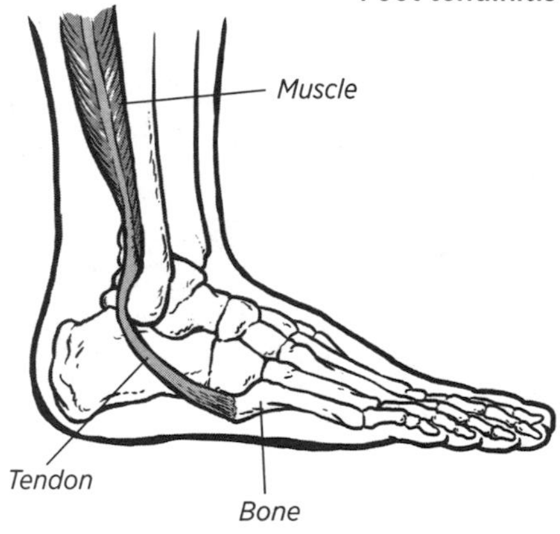

Orthotics to ensure proper foot motion, stretching and strengthening of the muscles and tendons in therapy, and PRP shots (see page 124) into the affected area are all used to reduce inflammation. However, prevention is the key. Good motion control shoes and a biomechanical evaluation by

Figure IV.14

Foot tendinitis

Muscle

Tendon

Bone

a sports doc may indicate that the correct orthotic can prevent the inflammation.

Morton's Foot

> **QUICK GUIDE: MORTON'S NEUROMA**
>
> **Symptoms:** Inflammation and pain between third and fourth toes.
>
> **How it occurred:** Chronic overpronation or supination.
>
> **What the doctor may do:** Physical examination. Gait analysis.
>
> **Likely treatment:** Full-length orthotic or orthotic adjustment. Cortisone injection. PRP injection. In extreme cases, surgery to remove swollen nerve.
>
> *NOTE: I dislike nerve removal because it causes a permanent loss of sensation in the affected area.*

In 1927, a physician named Dudley Joy Morton first described a foot where the second toe is longer than the big toe. Most folks have it the other way around, but fully 30 percent of the population have the foot that Morton described. Actually, people with Morton's foot have a normal-size big toe but a shorter first metatarsal than usual, and therefore the big toe starts farther back.

The reason this is important to runners is that we get our power to move forward off the base of that first metatarsal. Because the Morton's metatarsal is shorter, the foot is prone to overpronation and thereby stresses the bone. The overpronation can also inflame a nerve that lies between the second and third metatarsals; inflammation of the nerve is called neuroma.

Orthotics to take the stress off help both conditions; the orthotics must run the full length of the foot, and they must be flexible. The neuroma may need a cortisone injection. Rarely, surgeons remove that nerve if it is still painful; note, however, that with removal goes the ability to feel what your foot is doing. I have never had a case where proper orthotic control and injection did not make the neuroma pain go away, so in my experience, surgery is uncalled for.

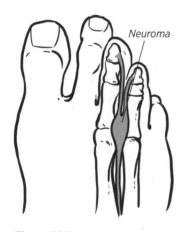

Neuroma

Figure IV.15

Morton's foot

Warts and Corns

> QUICK GUIDE: WARTS AND CORNS
>
> **Symptoms:** Warts: small, round lesions or bumps, sometimes painful. Corns: Hardened skin on high-friction areas.
>
> **How it occurred:** For warts, viral skin infection. For corns, friction from shoes and socks on skin.
>
> **What the doctor may do:** Physical examination.
>
> **Likely treatment:** For warts, commercial preparation. If not effective, a more powerful cure applied by the doctor. For corns, foot soaks followed by pumice stone.

Warts are the result of a viral skin infection. They are usually seen as small, round skin lesions that are sometimes painful. When scraped or abraded, they bleed. To get rid of them, foot soaks and abrasion of the wart are accompanied by the use of over-the-counter wart medications. You can buy wart freeze preparations at the drugstore that usually do a good job. Be sure to follow all the directions on the package. If the wart keeps coming back, see a doctor for a stronger freeze or a more powerful ointment that requires a prescription.

Corns and calluses are easily confused with warts. If you abrade a corn, it does not bleed. Corns and calluses are nothing more than hardened skin that builds up in high-friction areas like the bottom of the foot or over bony projections. A corn develops from a callus; the difference is that a corn has a mass of dead cells at its center. Corns appear on the toes and balls of the feet, and both corns and calluses can be painful. Treatment may include foot soaks to soften the skin followed by abrasion by the kind of pumice stone that you buy at the drugstore beauty counter. If this approach doesn't work, seek out a physician who can shave away the callus easily.

Marathon Feet

I coined this term years ago when covering first-time marathoners after their event. I would get a panicked phone call in the middle of the night: *"Doc, I just finished my first marathon yesterday, in 5:40:59!*

> QUICK GUIDE: MARATHON FEET
> **Symptoms:** Diffuse pain in feet the evening after a race.
> **How it occurred:** Running a marathon or half-marathon on a surface you did not train on or did not train for enough, shoe with insufficient cushion, not icing after event.
> **What the doctor may do:** Reassure you that this is normal.
> **Likely treatment:** Ice feet after event. Cushioned shoes. Train to respect the distance.

What a great time! I followed all your advice, but last night—starting at about 3 A.M.—both my feet started killing me. I could not walk! It hurt even to have my comforter rest on them! Is this normal? What is it? How can I prevent it?"

How cool to have finished and achieved that goal! And what these athletes are calling about is not at all uncommon and is actually the greatest complaint call I receive in the middle of the night after a first-time marathon finish. As with most injuries and conditions, this one is most easily prevented if understood.

What my middle-of-the-night callers are describing, if there is no bony tenderness or swelling, is what I call "marathon feet." In basic terms, it is inflamed soft tissues of the feet from the street pounding of 26.2 hard miles (although I have also seen it at the half-marathon, 13.1-mile distance). We most commonly see this in people who have trained on softer surfaces (like the reservoir track in New York City) than a paved road or who race in thin racing flats when they did not train in them. The inflamed soft tissues get more and more painful until it truly is hard to walk or even put a comforter over them.

Here are some things that you can do to prevent and/or treat marathon feet:

- Train on the same surface you plan to run on. If you are training for a marathon on roads, a treadmill or a soft track will not prepare your body for the pounding.
- Run in a well-cushioned shoe. Unless you plan on winning the race, racing flats or old, worn-out shoes that have lost their cushion will transmit a lot of road shock and give you

a case of marathon feet. Remember my "change shoes every 500 miles" rule so that your shoes are not too old or worn.

- After the race, when you have recovered sufficiently to be urinating normally (not experiencing "marathon kidney" as I discuss in conjunction with hyponatremia in "Avoiding Syncope and Hyponatremia" in Part I), you may take a nonsteroidal anti-inflammatory (such as aspirin or ibuprofen) unless your doctor has told you that you cannot due to a contraindication.
- Most important: Immediately upon returning home or to your hotel post-race, soak your feet for 15 minutes in an ice bath. This is the best way to avoid this middle-of-the-night pain.

Now, if you have pain the Monday after the event, 15-minute ice baths three times a day and an anti-inflammatory tablet (NSAID) may be necessary for two days to ease the inflammation. If you feel bony tenderness, see a doctor sooner rather than later; what you have may not be marathon feet but rather a stress or full fracture of a bone in your foot.

Dorsum Neuritis (Numb Toes)

QUICK GUIDE: DORSUM NEURITIS
Symptoms: Numb toes.
How it occurred: Shoes too tight on top of foot, pinching nerve.
What the doctor may do: Palpate area. Physical exam, including the use of a tuning fork to mimic symptoms. Doctor will look at your running shoes on your feet for tightness and proper fit. No need for X-ray or MRI.
Likely treatment: Lace shoes more loosely (see text). NSAID. Ice. If no relief, see doctor for nerve conduction study to rule out pinched nerve elsewhere.

Dorsum neuritis is a numbness in the toes. The story is always the same: "For the last year, when I go out for a run of four miles or more, the top of my foot hurts and I get a numb feeling that spreads to the tops of my second, third, and fourth toes." This is a problem I see in the office quite often, and my patients are relieved to know that just changing the tightness of the running shoe can make a difference.

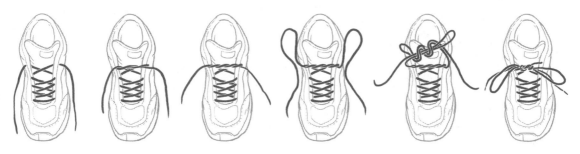

Figure IV.16

Nelson's knot

The pain and numbness are simply caused by pressure of the tongue and laces on the top of your foot that leads to impinging on a nerve. This nerve becomes inflamed as you run. Ice and elevation, along with an anti-inflammatory like Advil, Motrin, Aleve, or generic ibuprofen, should relieve your symptoms fairly quickly.

Now the issue is prevention. Be sure your running shoes fit properly. Did you get them fitted at the end of the day when your feet were more swollen? If not, they might be too small for you. Be sure they are one thumbnail's length longer than your longest toe and the toe box and heel counter fit properly. If you have orthotics, did you check the fit of the shoe with the orthotic in it?

Once you're sure the shoe is properly fitted, then lacing becomes the issue. Everyone, unfortunately, is an experiment unto her- or himself. There are plenty of shoelacing guides on the market to help you relieve the tightness.

Recently, a patient of mine taught me an outstanding knot that he borrowed from his sailing experience. It worked for him, and you may want to try "Nelson's Knot," which I named after him:

- Start the knot like you normally tie your shoes: Cross over and wrap one lace under the other to make a knot, and then wrap under and over again a second time; then pull.
- Create two "rabbit ears," one with each lace; cross over and wrap twice.
- Pull the ears tight.

Lisfranc Foot Injuries

Although the press regularly writes about Lisfranc season-ending injuries in professional football, runners get these injuries as well.

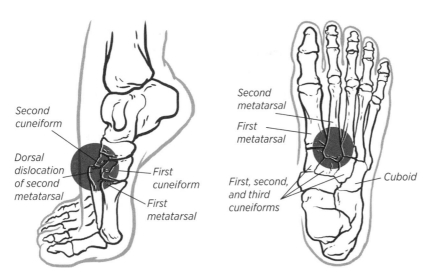

Figure IV.17A

Lisfranc foot injuries, side view

Figure IV.17B

Lisfranc foot injuries, top view

QUICK GUIDE: LISFRANC FOOT INJURIES

Symptoms: Pain in the midfoot.

How it occurred: Stepping in a pothole, twisting the foot and pushing off with force.

What the doctor may do: Complete medical history. Palpate the area. X-ray. MRI.

Likely treatment: If injury is a sprain, physical therapy. PRP injection has shown some promise in speeding healing. If injury is a fracture or dislocation, may require surgery. Cast or cast boot (non-weight-bearing), 6 weeks. Exogen bone stimulation. PRP injection for a fracture is still experimental but shows promise.

Lisfranc foot injuries occur in the midfoot. They're named after French surgeon Jacques Lisfranc de St. Martin, who in the 1800s, as a member of Napoleon's army, first described an injury sustained by mounted soldiers whose foot got caught in the saddle's stirrup as they got thrown off the horse. Nowadays, the injury happens when stepping into a pothole in the road, twisting the foot, or pushing off with force as a football lineman might do. These injuries can be ligament sprains, dislocations of the joints between the forefoot and midfoot, or fractures of the bones in the midfoot complex.

Anatomically, the Lisfranc joints are between the tarsometatarsal joints involving the cuneiform bone and metatarsal bones, as shown in the figure. Only a small percentage of Lisfranc injuries are fractures or dislocations; most are sprains involving the ligaments.

Diagnosis of this injury is simple when done by a sports doc who is familiar with the condition. After feeling the foot and twisting the midfoot (which would cause more pain if injured) and checking the pulse on top of the foot (because the artery there can sometimes be injured, too), the doctor will generally order standing and non-weight-bearing X-rays. However, Lisfranc injuries that are not fractures or dislocations will not be seen on X-ray. An MRI will then be ordered to check for a ligament sprain; the doctor will also look for bone marrow edema (fluid within the bone marrow) indicative of stress injury or stress fracture.

Treatment varies depending on whether the injury is a sprain or a fracture. A sprain will usually be treated in a cast or removable, non-weight-bearing cast boot (meaning that you cannot walk on the cast and will have to use crutches) for about 6 weeks. After removal, physical therapy and a very gradual return to sports usually take 8 to 12 weeks. Fractures and dislocations will require surgery with wires and/or screws to properly align the bones. The cast and non-weight-bearing postsurgery will last about 6 weeks, followed by another 6 to 8 weeks in a walking cast or cast boot. After that, you'll need physical therapy for another 8 to 12 weeks before getting back to sports.

This is an unfortunate timetable for runners who want to get back to running fast, but it must be followed for complete recovery. Better to know what is ahead if this happens to you (which I hope doesn't) than be surprised each step of the way.

Ankle Sprain, Ankle Break

The ankle is what I call "the great pretender" of the body, capable of ballooning threateningly after a minor sprain (tearing of ligaments—they attach bone to bone) or concealing a serious fracture behind nothing more than an unpleasant throb. As a sports medicine

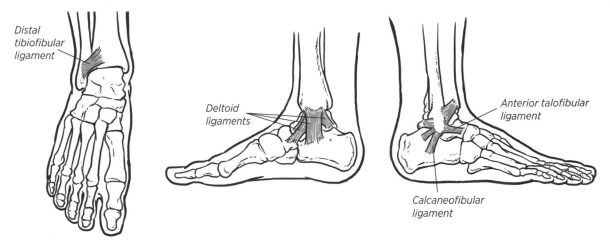

Figure IV.18A

Ankle sprain, top view

Figure IV.18B

Ankle sprain, medial view

Figure IV.18C

Ankle sprain, lateral view

QUICK GUIDE: ANKLE SPRAIN, ANKLE BREAK

Symptoms: Pain and swelling.

How it occurred: Inversion or eversion acute injury.

What the doctor may do: Palpate area. X-ray. MRI if ankle is not broken and is not getting better.

Likely treatment: If sprained, MICE (see text) and physical therapy; time down depends on severity of sprain. If broken, cast for 4 weeks followed by 4 weeks of physical therapy. Stretching and strengthening. PRP injection. Note that severe breaks require a few months for recovery.

physician, I've called them wrong both ways, finding just minor soft tissue damage after X-rays of patients I was ready to put into a cast and finding unexpected bone chips in others who were still managing daily workouts. It's chancy to assume, as so many of us do, that just because what's happening now feels like what happened last time, it *is* what happened last time.

Fortunately, fractures are far less common than sprains. And if a fracture is caught early, a couple of weeks in a cast usually permits rapid healing. Procrastinate, and the bone chip may migrate to someplace you don't want it and will have to come out with surgery if you expect to finally be rid of the pain. Then we're into real convalescence. So the rule is, know the difference. If there is any swelling after an ankle injury, please have it X-rayed.

But first things first.

Question 1: The instant you're hurt (usually miles from home in the middle of a workout), ask yourself, "Can I keep going?" If you can still run with the same stride, then go ahead. But if you start compensating, or if your biomechanics change even slightly, stop.

Question 2: "Why me?" Besides fate—being in the same place as a rock or pothole or curb—there is such a thing as a sprain-prone ankle. When an ankle patient comes to me, I always look first at the way his or her feet move. About 60 percent are ankle overpronators: people who land on the outside of their foot and come off on the inside, which makes them more vulnerable to an ankle twist. A good sports doc can make an orthotic that will flatten the footplants of these sprain-prone athletes and reduce this vulnerability.

Meantime, if it is a sprain, there's a lot more you can do than the usual RICE (rest, ice, compression, elevation). Ice is indispensable, of course, and should be nothing more elaborate than cubes in a Ziploc bag, with water to keep the temperature above 32 degrees so that you don't get freezer burn. Apply the ice two or three times a day for 20 minutes. And then instead of RICE, try MICE, substituting motion for rest. Sit cross-legged and pretend there is a pencil extending from your big toe. Now pretend to trace—with your foot, not just your toe—the capital letters of the alphabet from A to Z six times a day. This moves the ankle in every direction, bringing blood flow and more rapid healing. With the initial injury, this will be painful and the letters small. As you progress, the letters will get bigger and bigger.

The faster you get your ankle moving, the faster you will be back on the road, pain-free. You may run as soon as you can do so without changing your form. Running also brings in more blood flow for rapid healing.

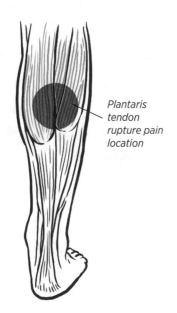

Plantaris tendon rupture pain location

Figure IV.19

Plantaris tendon

LEGS AND KNEES

Plantaris Tendon Rupture

> QUICK GUIDE: PLANTARIS TENDON RUPTURE
>
> **Symptoms:** Sharp, tightly pinpointed pain in midcalf, swelling, black-and-blue discoloration.
>
> **How it occurred:** Tear of brittle tendon in midcalf.
>
> **What the doctor may do:** Complete history. Physical exam. Gait analysis. Check lower extremity flexibility.
>
> **Likely treatment:** Will get better in 4–6 weeks. Physical therapy to reduce recovery time and increase flexibility. Orthotic or orthotic adjustment. No injections or immobilization needed. Resume exercise as soon as you can run without changing your running form to compensate for discomfort.

"Popped in the leg with a BB gun": That's what a plantaris tendon rupture feels like to most people. Or if you're on the tennis courts, as though you've been stung in the leg by a wild serve. But it always turns out there are no BBs or errant tennis balls anywhere near your calf, no excuse at all for it to start swelling, and no reason for it to eventually turn black and blue. Until recently, you would hobble off to a doctor and learn—incorrectly—that you had undoubtedly torn one of the major muscles in the area, probably requiring a long period of complete rest. Now we know better.

That's because a wispy, pencil-like muscle that runs down the middle of your lower leg is no longer a riddle to medical people. Called the "freshman nerve" because first-year medical students habitually mistake it for that, it's the plantaris muscle-tendon complex—like the appendix, one of evolution's leftovers. Once upon a time, the muscle might have helped you point your toe downward, but no more. The ones around it have taken over the job.

However, the plantaris muscle-tendon is still all connected up as if it had something to do, though all it does is grow gradually more and more brittle through the years until that day on the road when you come to a sudden halt as what feels like the worst pain of your life grips your calf. Sometimes called tennis leg, plantaris tendon rupture is more poetically referred to as "the disease of the aging athlete" because it's virtually unheard of in people under 40.

For years, even many sports medicine physicians dismissed plantaris rupture as a myth because no cases had ever been surgically proven. But a few years ago, researchers at the University of Miami published a paper confirming that the detailed investigation made possible by MRI had finally found two confirmed cases of plantaris tendon rupture. Too late for all those athletes who had been treated for more serious conditions. Not too late for you.

The good news is, the two ends of the rupture will shrivel up and go away—in a couple of weeks with a little physical therapy, a little longer without—and you'll never know the difference. The bad news? One more leg to go.

Shin Splints, Tibial Stress Syndrome, Exertional Compartment Syndrome

> QUICK GUIDE: SHIN SPLINTS
>
> **Symptoms:** Pain in shin.
>
> **How it occurred:** Overpronation (or, less likely, supination) and twisting of tibia.
>
> **What the doctor may do:** Palpate area. Gait analysis. X-ray. MRI. Compartment pressure test in some cases.
>
> **Likely treatment:** Calf stretches. Orthotic or orthotic adjustment. Physical therapy. Soft tissue deep massage of lower leg. Surgery if compartment syndrome is not resolved with physical therapy.

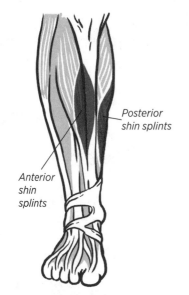

Posterior shin splints

Anterior shin splints

Figure IV.20

Shin splints

Shin splints encompass a number of disorders that include tibial stress syndrome, stress fractures, and exertional compartment syndrome. It is a condition in which some of your calf muscles wrap forward around your lower leg bone, usually at the inside flat part just about a third of the way up from the ankle, and it favors beginners, athletes coming back from a long layoff, and athletes upping their mileage as the weather gets better outside. Toe runners are constantly told they're perfect candidates for the condition, but they're not. It's brought on by a combination of overly tight calf muscles and not what the foot does when it lands, but *after* it lands.

Picture a pronating runner with flat feet—the classic shin splint candidate. Airborne, his or her foot acquires a subtle curve where the rest of us have higher arches. Then the foot lands, flattens out, and as the ankle rolls inward (pronates), the shin bone or tibia is forced to twist slightly in the opposite or outward direction. Over and over and over. So anything attached to it—like the calf muscle—is going to be yanked over and over and over, too. That spells shin splints.

If this is the pain you feel, you're lucky because it can be treated with ice, over-the-counter anti-inflammatories, and a proper orthotic. Ignore these early signs at your own peril. The shin bone is covered with a membrane called the periosteum, which can in turn become inflamed from the muscle's tugging. And eventually, of course, a twisting tibia is headed for a stress fracture.

The single most effective step is to stop the foot rolling, and only a proper orthotic can do that. The orthotic must be soft and flexible, and it must control the forefoot on takeoff.

Loosening the calf muscles also cuts your shins some slack. Try the stretches recommended here. More is better. You cannot do these too much.

If you have done the exercises conscientiously and still have no relief, you may need some physical therapist's hands to do soft tissue work to loosen your calf muscles.

Still not better? Ask your sports physician the following questions:

- Is shin splints the correct diagnosis? Do I have a stress fracture or compartment syndrome that is not resolving with the current treatment?
- Are my orthotics controlling my forefoot when I am on the ball of my feet (80 percent of the time when you run)?

Shin splints should resolve with two weeks if you have the correct orthotics and your stretching is compulsively done.

Of course, as a Running Doc I always think of horses, not zebras, first when I hear hoofbeats (in medicine, a *zebra* is an unexpected diagnosis and comes from a lesson by Dr. Theodore Woodward, who said to his medical students in Baltimore, "When you hear hoofbeats behind you, don't expect to see a zebra"). So when I am looking for the horse first, by far the most common cause of shin splints is forefoot pronation and inadequate stretching, and I do see patients every day who "think" their orthotics are working. When I correct the orthotic, the pain goes away. So first get your orthotics checked by your sports physician (or see your sports physician about orthotics if you don't have them).

The second most common cause is tibial stress syndrome, on the way to stress fracture, again caused by tibial twisting when landing (again due to pronation and again corrected by good orthotics and calf stretching). But if orthotics and flexibility are OK, it is time to look for the zebra!

Now we may in fact be dealing with a rare condition (rare because I suspect not many look for it) called intermittent or exertional compartment syndrome, which mimics shin splints and sometimes does not respond to the preceding treatments, even when done properly. The condition is called intermittent because it goes away in a few hours after the exertion, with rest. That means, of course, that it is not usually there when you walk into the doctor's office.

It's called compartment syndrome because it is named for the rigid tubes, or compartments, within which nature has seen fit to encapsulate the muscles of the lower leg. Now this would be of no concern if the compartments gave the muscles plenty of room to function. But they don't always do so. Runners have a way of developing those lower leg muscles, and if they happen to have inherited stingy leg-muscle compartments, the squeeze could be on as blood flows to the hardworking legs and the muscles swell with additional liquid. As they do, the first thing that begins to go as the muscle is squeezed against the compartment walls is the veins' ability to carry off the blood as quickly as it's coming in. But that doesn't stop the arteries, whose superior pressure keeps injecting more and more blood into the muscles anyway.

In extreme cases, the condition becomes a total stalemate, with no more new blood coming in, no more old blood getting out. The result is unsurprising: Tissue dies. You can lose use of the muscle altogether. In extreme cases, timely surgery is necessary; this consists of nothing more than two small incisions on the surface and a release

Calf Muscle Stretches

Figure IV.21

Gastroc stretch

Standing about 2 feet from a tree or wall, lean into it with your good foot forward, your back straight, and the affected foot behind you, heel on the ground. Hold for 20 seconds. Repeat 10 times. Switch legs and repeat.

Figure IV.22

Soleus stretch

Repeat the gastroc stretch, this time with the knee of the affected foot slightly bent. Remember: Heel on the ground.

(slice) underneath the compartment to allow everything to expand properly without pain.

Fortunately, most exertional compartment syndrome cases are not extreme and just mimic shin splints that won't go away. Either very strong hands in physical therapy or elective surgery is the cure.

I have seen the results over and over. With proper care from a good physical therapist (or, in the extreme, within six months after the surgical procedure), I have seen runners fully recover; cosmetically, one cannot even tell that they have had the surgery.

Diagnosis is the key. Nowadays, there are two ways to find out if this rare condition has you complaining that your shin splints just won't go away. Some radiologists are now doing an MRI immediately after a hard workout while you still have the symptoms. Although a controversial method of diagnosis, it is gaining more and more acceptance. Most surgeons, however, rely on the gold standard test of measuring compartment pressures in the office. This test inserts a small needle into the compartment before a workout and just after while symptoms remain. The needle is attached to a little gizmo that measures and reads out the compartment pressure. The change in measured pressures is diagnostic and justifies the surgical fix.

One new interesting cause of this syndrome is being discussed by sports doctors around the country. High school athletes who supplement with creatine seem to have an increased risk for this syndrome. Creatine is an organic acid that helps supply energy to the muscle cells in the body, and it is used in the form of creatine phosphate to "bulk up" in many sports because it is legal and easily obtained at health food stores. Research has shown that there do not appear to be any long-term side effects, but creatine does add water molecules to muscle tissue, which makes muscles feel "bulky" and "fluffy." If you have decreased space in the muscle compartment, now the muscle is bigger in that space and therefore a risk.

Professional athletes have essentially stopped using creatine phosphate supplements because the increased bulk caused by the water molecules makes muscle tears heal at a slow rate, which translates to increased time on the disabled list. And no one wants that.

So if exertional compartment syndrome is your problem, get a diagnosis and get it treated. I just wonder how many runners who have been treated for chronic shin splints are simply giving up in disgust, when in reality all they needed was a proper diagnosis and a surgical repair to be back on the road again, pain-free . . . forever!

Stair Toe Raises for Aching Calves

Figure IV.23

Stair toe raises I

Stand with the balls of your feet on a stair, with the midfoot and heels hanging back over the edge. Point your feet straight forward. During a 10-second period, slowly raise your heels over the step, then lower them below the step, and then go back to the horizontal. Repeat 10 times.

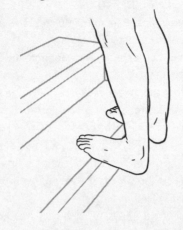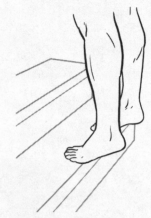

Figure IV.24

Stair toe raises II

Same as Raise I, but with toes pointing inward.

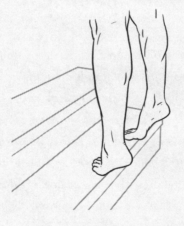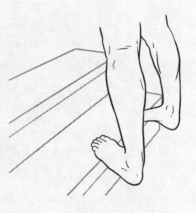

Figure IV.25

Stair toe raises III

Same as Raise I, but with toes pointing outward.

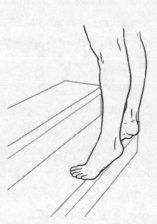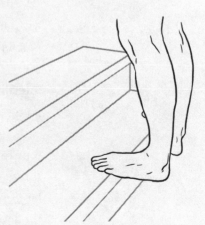

Runner's Knee

QUICK GUIDE: RUNNER'S KNEE

Symptoms: Pain going up and down stairs, stiffens after sitting through a movie, no history of trauma.

How it occurred: Overpronation and kneecap pulling off line. Tight lateral connective tissue around knee. Weak middle quad muscle.

What the doctor may do: Full knee exam, with doctor pushing down on kneecap to test for grinding. Middle quad strength test. Gait analysis.

Likely treatment: Orthotic or orthotic adjustment. Quad extension exercise. Physical therapy. Raise seat on bike. Resume exercise as soon as you can run without changing your running form due to pain from injury. Severe cases respond well to cortisone injection under kneecap. PRP injection.

NOTE: Surgery for lateral release is not recommended; area will heal with scar tissue, causing worse pain than before.

Johnny is a 62-year-old retired accountant living in Miami Beach. "Doc, my right knee hurts when I walk down the ramp from my lodge seats at the horse track. Both knees stiffen up when I sit in a movie theatre. My doctor told me I have 'runner's knee,' but I have never run! What's up?"

Jane is a 34-year-old housewife raising a pair of boys, ages 4 and 8. "Both knees bother me going up and down stairs, Doc, and they stiffen when I finally get to sit and read a book. My doctor says I have 'runner's knee,' but I don't have time to run! Is he wrong?"

Runner's knee does not happen only to runners. It is a condition with many names: chondromalacia patella, anterior knee syndrome, patella femoral disorder, and, of course, runner's knee. It is seen every day by sports doctors, orthopedic surgeons, family doctors, and internists. Understanding the real cause makes treatment easy and pain relief possible in a short period of time.

When it comes to runner's knee, biology is destiny. Anyone whose foot rolls inward (overpronation) during a stride is a candidate, but the real high-risk frontrunners are people with extremely flat feet; a large, pronating forefoot; or a Morton's foot (a foot where the second toe is longer than the first; see page 134), causing an exaggerated rolling in, or pronation. Your parents gave you those feet, not your sport, your activity, or a specific injury.

Of all the aches and pains that one can get, this one's probably the easiest to get rid of. If you were doing some serious running mileage over the summer, maybe getting ready for a fall marathon, or pain came on "all of a sudden" without any apparent injury and your knee suddenly started to get sore when you walked up and down stairs, or you felt stiff when you were sitting in a movie, you most probably have it. You could have come down with it when you were 12, or 65. And the treatment, which is not complicated or extensive, is the same for everybody from kids to grandparents.

It all starts with the kneecap. In a perfect world, your kneecap rides up and down in a V-shaped groove that sits just behind it as you walk, run, or cycle. More typically, however, your foot rolls in, or pronates, as you move from heel strike to toe-off, and the kneecap ends up scraping along one side of the groove instead of sliding smoothly up and down the middle. The cartilage there doesn't much like getting sandpapered down that way, nor does the back of the kneecap, which begins to weep fluid that in turn produces a feeling of stiffness. And though runners have named the condition, it crops up often in nonathletes, as well as among cyclists and in cleated-shoe sports like soccer and baseball whose footwear can put sideways torque on the knee.

Physicians can diagnose it from the other side of the room: joint hurts, no particular injury caused it, worst going upstairs and downstairs (or walking down an incline, which tightens the thigh muscle, pulling the kneecap down into the groove and causing a painful rubbing), stiffens after sitting a while, feels like it needs to be stretched. That settles it.

Despite what you may have read, arthroscopic surgery is not the immediate answer. (Arthroscopic surgery is a minimally invasive procedure where the surgery is performed through an arthroscope—an instrument that pokes into the area through a small hole. The advantages over traditional open surgery, where a large incision is

LEGS & KNEES

Time for a Quad Job

If you're suffering from runner's knee, strengthening the medial quad muscle will help hold your kneecap in the correct position. But to avoid further injury, you should not perform traditional quad exercises. Instead, do these terminal extension exercises. Follow the instructions carefully, making sure not to exceed the recommended amount of motion.

1. Sit up on a desk or high surface, stick your leg out straight, drop it about six inches, and support it with a chair or stool.

2. Wrap your ankle with a weight bag made for the purpose, or fill a gym bag or duffel with weights—books, soup cans, whatever—and strap it to the lower leg. See the next step for the correct amount of weight to use.

3. Lift only the last six inches (about 30 degrees) to full extension, hold for three seconds, and then come slowly back down. Do 5 sets of 10 reps each day, with just enough weight that you get to 5 or 6 on that fifth set and have to stop. Can't get there? Take out some weight. Can do all 10? Add a book or some soup.

4. If you are at a gym, use the leg extension weight machine. Do one leg at a time. Hold your one leg out to full extension with the weight. Then drop your leg down six inches, and put the pin in the machine to lock it at that point. (Every weight machine is different. Have your gym instructor show you how to set the machine to limit your range of weight training.) Bending your knee too far will bring the kneecap into the groove and grind it, leading to damage to the knee as you strengthen the muscles! Again, 5 sets of 10 repetitions with as much weight as it takes to get to 5 or 6 on the fifth set.

5. If you're a cyclist, raise the seat on your bike a bit higher than normal. As you pedal, that will help put you into the "good" range of motion, rather than continuing to abuse your kneecap.

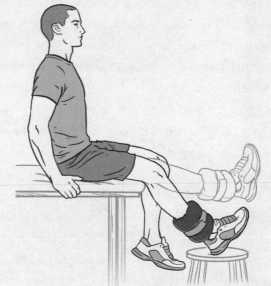

Figure IV.26

Limited quad extensions for runner's knee

made, are less muscle trauma and quicker healing.) Surgery helps perhaps 1 out of 100 sufferers. One favored operation consists of mechanically smoothing the rubbing surface of the kneecap; this treatment can give relief for six months or so, but unless your biomechanics have changed, it's a borrowed-time fix. Cutting the retinaculum (the connective tissue holding the kneecap in place) to loosen it in the groove, another surgical approach, is also only temporary. It eventually scars down tighter than it was before. Sooner or later, you're back where you started.

A proper orthotic (an arch support made by a qualified podiatrist that goes into your shoe and changes your foot motion from rolling to going straight) is the single most important step because it will prevent the roll that caused the scraping in the first place. The good news is that once you start wearing the orthotic, your knee cooperates quickly: The patella cartilage that's been rubbed down is able to regenerate and heal itself. Just give it the chance.

But orthotics alone won't do it. You need your other ally, the medial quad, which is the muscle in the front inside of your thigh that's supposed to hold the kneecap in the center of the groove. The stronger your medial quad muscle is, the better it can do its job. There's a rub, however: The common exercise recommended to strengthen this muscle is the leg extension, but as you do the routine, the quad also pulls the kneecap back down into the groove and grinds it up some more. No good. Instead, you need to perform the terminal extension exercises shown here ("Time for a Quad Job," page 152), which limit the motion to the last 6 inches of extension. Do them daily until the pain disappears, then twice weekly. And do both legs, please, even if only one leg hurts. Your knees are a matched pair, and what's already happened on one side is a good bet for the other someday.

Knee sleeves and elastic bandages (such as Ace bandages) are out. Think about it. If you compress the kneecap, every motion will press it into the groove. Keep it loose and free.

Some patients benefit from a corticosteroid injection under the kneecap, and some do even better with the new PRP injection protocol

What Knee Brace Should I Buy for My Runner's Knee?

I rarely recommend a brace for true runner's knee. Once you understand the process, you will see why. Runner's knee is really a wearing down of the cartilage in the back of the kneecap. It comes from improper lateral tracking of the V-shaped back of the patella in the groove so that it starts to wear down from a smooth surface to a rough sandpaper-like substance. That is why the telltale signs occur of pain going up and down stairs, a feeling of the knee giving way (though it never does), and clicking. The quadriceps muscle contracts (especially going down stairs), it pulls the kneecap down into the groove, and you feel pain. When the kneecap is rough, it weeps fluid into the closed knee joint space and your knee feels stiff when you sit for a long time; you may feel pain behind the knee because that is the weakest point in this closed knee joint space and it pushes out there like a balloon.

The good news is that if you can fix the tracking and move the kneecap into the center of the groove, the back of the kneecap smooths out and the symptoms resolve. Although braces may keep the kneecap in the center, every one I have seen, no matter what they say in their advertising, pushes or holds the kneecap down in the groove with too much pressure, and that pressure continues the grinding that causes the pain in the first place. Better to be as free as possible and fix your body so that it no longer grinds that kneecap laterally.

The kneecap is riding laterally due to a weak medial quad, tightened lateral connective tissue holding it there, and probable overpronation. A better gift to yourself than a brace would be evaluation by a good sports physician, adoption of full-length flexible orthotics custom-made for your feet, and physical therapy to stretch that lateral connective tissue along with a program of terminal knee extensions.

If you follow this advice, within four weeks your present to yourself will be running pain-free, brace free.

(see page 124), but those remedies are employed only for those patients not rapidly feeling improvement with orthotics and exercise.

So you've worn your orthotics, you've done your exercises faithfully, and the pain is gone. Are you cured? No. You could have your orthotics superglued to your feet for a year, and if you took them off, after 365 days and 1 minute your inherited biomechanics would resume, and eventually the pain would return right along with it. So make these exercises a part of your weekly routine, keep wearing your orthotics, and you can rid yourself of this unnecessary pain forever.

Iliotibial Band Syndrome

QUICK GUIDE: ILIOTIBIAL BAND SYNDROME

Symptoms: Pain on lateral side of knee or hip a mile or two into run. Never have pain from first step.

How it occurred: Friction of tight iliotibial band rubbing at hip and/or knee.

What the doctor may do: Palpate ITB. Gait analysis for overpronation. X-ray and MRI not needed.

Getting back to running: Stretching. Foam roller. "The Stick." Orthotic or orthotic adjustment. If a small bursa has formed around Gerdy's Tubercle, cortisone injection into the bursa. PRP if cortisone is ineffective. You can run through IT pain as long as it does not change your running form.

NOTE: Surgery should be last resort. In all my years of practice, I have seen only one case that required surgery to remove the bursa around Gerdy's Tubercle.

Iliotibial band syndrome, also called ITB friction syndrome, inflicts sharp knee or hip pain on a wide range of sufferers: ballet dancers, football players, and—yes—runners and walkers. Brought on by a sudden increase in training mileage or even a single unusually long workout, it's nothing more than an irritation of a band of connective tissue that goes from the hip (the iliac crest) to the shin bone (the tibia). Hence, iliotibial.

The band could go about its business of stabilizing a runner's foot during footstrike if only it didn't have to pass over two impediments—a bony projection (called Gerdy's tubercle) on the outside of your knee, and another diffuse bony protuberance (which has no name) on the hip—every time your leg is bent and straightened again. Loose ITBs slide harmlessly past the two obstructions. Tight ones rub against them, get irritated, and react with a sharp pain on the outside of the knee or hip that usually does not become bothersome until a couple of miles into your workout.

In the spring, my waiting room fills with suddenly ambitious spring trainers who find, practically overnight, that they can't run

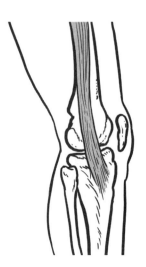

Figure IV.27

Iliotibial band

Stretching a Tight Iliotibial Band

Figure IV.28

ITB primary stretch

Lie on your back, bring your left knee to your shoulder, and push your knee over to the right shoulder with the palm of your left hand. Hold for 20 seconds, and repeat five times. Then do your right knee. Perform three times each day and also before workouts.

Figure IV.29

ITB standing stretch

With your arm against a wall or pole, slowly stretch toward the wall or pole with the other arm supporting your trunk. Do this whenever you see a wall not doing anything!

very far. You can diagnose this from across the room: "Doc, the pain starts a few miles into the run, not at the beginning, and sometimes I wake up with it the next morning after a long run." They've taken a few days off, to no avail. They've switched to their bicycles but gotten no relief (they're feeling the same rubbing during cycling).

The really determined ones have scanned a couple of ITB articles, and now they're sitting there girding themselves for, one, a long layoff; two, a local steroid injection; or, three, surgery. In my opinion none of that's necessary, though you might not know it from the number of athletes advised to try at least one of the three remedies. Surgery is a last resort, and a long layoff won't do anything to loosen a tight ITB.

Figure IV.30

Using a roller to stretch out the ITB

Lie sideways on the foam roller. Roll the ITB area back and forth to loosen it up.

Figure IV.31

Using "The Stick" to stretch out the ITB

While comfortably seated, grab "The Stick" at each end and roll it back and forth over the ITB to loosen it.

But simple stretching will work wonders, and that's all the injury usually requires. Whether you were born with an abnormally tight ITB or stiffened it with exercise (the band contains a very small amount of muscle tissue), the key to a cure is to get some slack back into it. Then it won't rub. Ice and an oral anti-inflammatory will help get rid of the pain, but only a supple ITB can keep the condition from returning.

The simplest stretch is to lie on your back, bring your left knee up to your shoulder, and push your knee over to the right shoulder with the palm of your left hand. Hold for 20 seconds, and repeat five times. Then do your right knee. Do this exercise at least three times a day in addition to making it part of your preworkout routine (yes, you can continue to exercise), and you'll probably see results in about a week. When the condition clears up, just use the stretch whenever you can; more is better!

There's a second simple exercise to stretch the band out that I also recommend. Stand at arm's length from a wall with your feet together. Keeping your feet in place and your arm extended, slowly stretch your hips toward the wall, hold for a few seconds, and then return to a standing position. Turn around, put your other hand on the wall, and repeat. Simple. Do this one often, and you will find the suppleness of your ITB coming along nicely.

For most who have faithfully tried these exercises without relief, stretching is just not enough. A foam roller, which you can get at marathon expos or online, is a good addition to stretch out the band. The roller is nothing more than a short log made of dense, lightweight foam. The roller is about 4 inches in diameter, and all you need to do is lie on it and roll the affected area back and forth on top of it. You can also try "The Stick," which has a series of small-diameter rollers on a spindle; you grab the stick at each end and roll it back and forth over the affected area. Again, more is better; you cannot do this too much, only too little.

If you are still not better, you may have been blessed with really tight connective tissue. In that case, not only will you need physical therapy, but also some therapy centers now have a new machine called a "Powerplate." Most professional teams have this gizmo, and some celebrities like Madonna are said to have purchased one. This expensive machine works by vibration while you stretch on it, and I have seen people who were so tight you never thought you'd get them stretched out look like Gumby after four short weeks of stretching on this machine three times a week!

Some people develop what I call an adventitial bursal sac right around Gerdy's tubercle. This fluid-filled structure can get inflamed from running; a simple cortisone shot right there has done miracles for some patients. Don't be afraid of the cortisone, as it stays locally and there are no systemic effects.

Last but not least, when you are running, the ITB stretches when you overpronate and releases (contracts) when your foot is in the air. Just as a stretched rubber band comes back shorter when released, so does the ITB. If you are using an orthotic to correct your forefoot position, and the orthotic is flexible, you don't need to change it (or *them*, most likely, because both feet will probably be overpronating). If your orthotic is made of a hard material that ends midfoot, however, chances are you need to get a different one that works while you are running because you spend 70 to 80 percent of your time on your forefoot.

If none of this provides relief, ask your sports physician the following questions:

- Do I really have ITB syndrome, or is it something else?
- Have I developed a new bursa at Gerdy's tubercle that would respond to a steroid injection or PRP?
- Am I an overpronator, and are my orthotics correcting for this?

If in fact you do have ITB syndrome, however, and you follow my advice, you will be pain-free within four weeks! Promise.

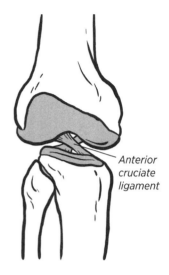

Figure IV.32A

Anterior cruciate ligament, close view

Anterior Cruciate Ligament

QUICK GUIDE: ANTERIOR CRUCIATE LIGAMENT

Symptoms: Pain, swelling, laxity (looseness and a feeling that the knee is going to give way).

How it occurred: A traumatic twist and rotation of knee.

What the doctor may do: Complete knee exam. X-ray to look for break or bone chip. MRI if needed to seal diagnosis.

Likely treatment: If you don't want or absolutely do not need surgery (per your physician), a knee brace for stability (running can continue). Reconstructive surgery is usually indicated, especially if you feel unstable. A torn ACL will not heal on its own, due to insufficient blood supply in ligament.

Too many doctors—even sports specialists—are still advising older amateur athletes that when it comes to injury of the knee's anterior cruciate ligament (ACL), they should just settle for whatever physical

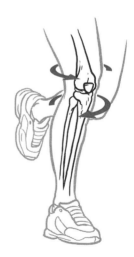

Figure IV.32B

Anterior cruciate ligament, extended view

therapy can accomplish. The penalty: Either give up most everything that's rough on the knee—tennis, soccer, football, skiing, track and field—or wear a brace and accept a reduced level of play. Fine if sports and fitness are a cursory pastime, but for a lot of people they're not.

The ACL is one of two ligaments that hold the knee joint's top bone, the femur, to the bottom bone, the tibia. It's also a major stabilizer, keeping the tibia from sliding forward into space. Trouble usually comes when an athlete's lower leg wants to rotate but the foot is fixed and won't let it, as when your ski suddenly gets caught in the snow. The ACL, abnormally taut from the position anyway, can sprain or tear. No sport is risk-free, but running, pivoting, and jumping competitions like football, soccer, and track and field—plus skiing—are the worst enemies of this balky tissue.

Why balky? Because it seems so easy to injure and so hard to fix. One 22-year-old patient of mine was carrying a mattress down the stairs on moving day when she twisted her leg and *pop!* went the ACL. A top track-and-field athlete of 50 felt hers go while she was weightlessly airborne during a javelin throw.

The young woman chose to have a minor procedure to clean up the motion-restricting ragged ends of the ligament. She faced a three-month road of physical therapy and a lifetime of caution. The track star's surgery was more complex, involving replacement of the ACL using tissue taken from the knee, and her recovery naturally was longer. But it was also more complete.

At first, however, she doubted she even had a choice. Just days after flying back from the Masters Nationals in Spokane where the injury had occurred, the woman sat in my sports medicine office despondent at the news that an MRI had confirmed her ligament tear. She figured it was the classic career-ending injury.

What she didn't figure on hearing was that she was a perfect candidate for surgery that would put her sports career back on track. First, microsurgery with the arthroscope works best on the knee because the joint has sufficient space for the scope to slip easily among the bones, cartilage, and other tissues. Second, whether or not you're a candidate for replacement ACL surgery depends not so much on your age or athletic status as on the work you're willing to do during the nine or so months of physical therapy that follow.

Distal Hamstring Bursitis

QUICK GUIDE: DISTAL HAMSTRING BURSITIS
Symptoms: Pain in back of leg at top of calf.
How it occurred: Hamstring tightness and friction, causing bursa to form and become inflamed.
What the doctor may do: Complete history. Physical exam.
Likely treatment: Hamstring stretches. Physical therapy with cross-frictional massage, electrical stimulation, and ultrasound. Cortisone injection into bursa (not into the tendon!) to relieve symptoms. If not successful, then PRP injection, which requires 2 weeks to relieve symptoms.

The hamstring muscle inserts at the back of the top of the calf on both sides. Sometimes a bursa there can get inflamed. The sure cure: cortisone or PRP injection (see page 124). Simple, fast, and can be done within three days of a marathon. You will be running pain-free soon thereafter.

Proximal Hamstring Tendinitis/Tendinosis

QUICK GUIDE: PROXIMAL HAMSTRING TENDINOSIS
Symptoms: Pain in the butt at the bone, especially while sitting.
How it occurred: Overly tight hamstring muscle, overpronation or supination pulling hamstring off line.
What the doctor may do: Complete medical history indicating no specific injury point. Palpate area. MRI.
Likely treatment: Physical therapy. Electrical stimulation. Ice massage. Orthotic or orthotic adjustment. Cortisone injection around tendon, *not in it*. PRP injection. You can run as long as the condition does not change your running form. You may need to shorten stride and slow down to maintain running form.

Ligament Tears, Meniscal Tears: Do I Need Surgery?

Before we discuss the merits of surgery to repair ligament tears, let's set the most important ground rule: Never, and I mean never, have a surgical procedure without a second opinion from someone you trust. By this I do not mean a trusted family friend; I mean a sports medicine doctor or practitioner with great credentials in your local community. It is always good to hear other opinions and then weigh the options. Most insurance policies cover this process, so avail yourself of the opportunity. Be careful, as I always say, when considering opinions, and also be careful not to immediately embrace the opinion you want to hear because it may not be the most learned. Try to be objective and informed.

That said, I am always a little troubled when the outcome from a normal exam leads to a diagnosis of surgery. My motto is, never treat the MRI. Good physicians treat the patient. That is, they order MRIs to confirm a diagnosis, not to find one. There are plenty of times that the MRI film may appear to reveal a ligament tear even though the physical exam is normal, and sure enough when the surgeon opens the area and takes a direct look at it, he or she finds that there is no tear and no need for surgery.

A much more sensitive and reliable test is one that we use on the sidelines at football games. If there is a knee with a suspected meniscal tear, we ask the patient to squat down like a duck. If there is no pain when squatting like a duck and also when walking like a duck, chances are very likely there is no meniscus tear and no need for surgery.

If you have a negative "duck walk" test, I suggest you see a sports medicine physician familiar with runners. You need a real diagnosis based on your physical exam, not your film.

If you are "duck walk" positive and the film indicates a tear, you probably do need arthroscopic surgery. Make sure it is performed by someone who treats runners regularly. If you do, your running career should resume pain-free one month postop after some good therapy.

Medial and lateral collateral ligament sprains (on the inside and outside of the knee) rarely need surgery and do well with rehab. Anterior and posterior ligament tears are rare in runners, but they do usually need surgery if symptomatic, and (I am sorry to say) have long rehabs. Lateral meniscus tears sometimes need surgery, whereas medial meniscus tears almost certainly do need arthroscopy because the medial meniscus is a knee stabilizer and is needed intact to prevent your knee from giving way.

Bottom line: Get an opinion from someone you trust. And worry not; no matter what the surgery, you will run again in time.

This is a common problem among runners and yet one often not recognized accurately enough to get a resolved outcome in an efficient manner. Typically, this problem starts over a year before the patient presents to a doctor's office with tendinitis. It is an inflammation of the tendon that attaches the hamstring muscle to the bone in your butt. The initial tendinitis occurred due to your running motion pulling the hamstring off its exact biomechanical line. If you are an overpronator, that is the cause of its pulling off line.

The hamstring tendon gets its strength and flexibility from the exquisite pattern and organization of its fibers—they are lined up in parallel. Now, to understand what's going on, you first need to know that every body structure undergoes constant remodeling, but at different rates. For example, your cornea remodels in 24 hours. Your hamstring, however, remodels more slowly. If the remodeling takes place in an environment of inflammation (tendinitis), the tendon remodels with the pattern every which way, not the pattern of exquisite parallel fibers. This new tendon is weak, swollen, and more prone to tear than it was before. The pain just will not go away. Physicians call this condition tendinosis, as opposed to tendinitis.

Getting rid of hamstring tendinosis requires that you follow to the letter this entire protocol:

- Get a custom running orthotic, and wear it full-time until the tendon is remodeled completely (maybe six months). Refrain from simply buying a stability shoe, which is equivalent to buying glasses over the counter; it won't do the job. Get the orthotic.

- Get physical therapy. A therapist needs to do "cross-frictional massage" across the tendon, which will bring in more blood flow to speed remodeling. Do not trust this to a massage therapist. This tendon is weak, and physical therapists are specifically trained in how much that tendon can stand without ripping (a major problem if this happens!).

- Perform hamstring curls six days a week at home. Lie on your bed facedown with your feet hanging off the end. Using no more than a five-pound ankle weight, lift your ankle toward

LEGS & KNEES

your butt, hold for three seconds, and then slowly lower your ankle back down to full extension. This works the entire muscle.

Note: No runner should ever do seated hamstring curls at the gym; these work only the belly of the muscle, and when you go out to run, you will tear some other part of the muscle.

In addition to this protocol, a corticosteroid injection may be useful to speed the healing process; you'll have to ask your physician about it. Note that the injection cannot be placed within the tendon as corticosteroids cause tendon weakness and lead to a rupture.

An alternative to the corticosteroid injection is the new PRP procedure (see page 124) using your body's own platelets, which causes healing factors to remodel faster. The speed of healing is the main advantage of PRP over a corticosteroid injection, but note that PRP is much more expensive. My advice? If your doctor offers PRP, take it. If not, go with the corticosteroid and rest easy; it will do the job, too, in time.

Do not get frustrated if you do not feel better quickly. This condition did not settle in overnight, and it will take an equally long time to get rid of it (unless you are able to take advantage of PRP, which significantly reduces healing time). Keep this in mind, and know that if you follow the advice given here and get rid of the pain,

Hamstring Curls at Home

Figure IV.33

Hamstring curls for proximal hamstring tendinitis

Lie facedown on your bed with your feet off the end. Strap a weight of five pounds or less to one ankle. Lift ankle to butt, hold three seconds, and lower. Repeat 10 times, then do other leg.

it will be gone for good unless you stop the curls and the stretching and don't wear your orthotics!

Unresolved Quadriceps Pain

QUICK GUIDE: UNRESOLVED QUADRICEPS PAIN
Symptoms: Pain in thigh muscle that does not resolve with physical therapy.
How it occurred: Calcium deposit in the muscle (myositis ossificans), midfemur stress syndrome, or a deep vein clot.
What the doctor may do: For myositis ossificans, palpation and X-ray to look for calcium deposit. For midfemur stress syndrome, X-ray, MRI. For deep vein clot, venous ultrasound.
Likely treatment: For myositis ossificans, physical therapy, ultrasound, stretching. Cortisone shot or by mouth. Warm soaks. For midfemur stress syndrome, rest, physical therapy. Exogen bone stimulation. PRP injection. For deep vein clot, anticoagulants. Rest.

Quadriceps pain (pain in the thigh muscle) is most often due to a muscle tear of some kind: a microtear, a strain, a muscle pull, tendinitis. All of these types of injuries that involve muscle tears should begin to heal within four weeks of therapy. If with ongoing therapy you are not better and you cannot attribute the pain to a specific injury, there may be something else going on. Let's discuss what long bouts of thigh pain could be and how to find out whether one of them fits you.

Myositis ossificans, a rare condition in which bone forms within the muscle, is something we see after a strong bruise in the thigh. What happens is that the "bruise" actually releases blood; it looks black and blue initially. Calcium then deposits there (doctors take an X-ray and see calcium in the muscle and/or soft tissue to make this diagnosis), and lots of therapy, ultrasound, and stretching are needed to get rid of the pain. Sometimes this condition takes 8 to 12 months to improve. It does feel better with ice and/or Icy Hot cream or wet heat (use a warm wet towel, or soak in the bath), which breaks down old blood and calcium deposits.

Midfemur stress syndrome or stress fracture is by far the most common "second- or third-opinion" diagnosis I seem to make to patients presenting with a history of no specific injury, long-term pain, and lengthy therapy without resolution of the pain. I first start with an X-ray to see if there is a healing stress fracture (signs of healing can be seen on a plane X-ray; the doctor looks to see whether a fracture callus has formed, which is a mass of heterogeneous tissue that grows around the fracture site during healing). Usually the X-ray is negative, and we need to proceed to an MRI, looking for the characteristic appearance of stress reaction or stress fracture. There is more than one way to treat this condition, and you need to have a discussion with your physician as to how fast you want to be back and which treatment plan will work best for you. Recovery could involve crutches and complete rest for 4 weeks followed by physical therapy, or it could follow a simpler plan of no-weight-bearing exercise; a prescription of flexible, full-length orthotics worn full-time for 12 to 16 weeks; and physical therapy. But continuing to exercise without caring for the problem will just keep it going, like blowing on a burning ember. Be sure also to get a bone density test to see if you are osteoporotic.

Vascular (blood circulation) problems have sometimes presented to physicians in unusual ways. Sometimes a deep vein clot can mimic a quad strain. Usually there is a history of sitting for a long time, as on a long flight, associated with this condition. The usual symptom is discomfort behind the knee, but I recently saw a patient with this same quad pain misdiagnosed as a "quad strain," and it had been with him since a flight from Australia to New York City seven months prior! The test is a venous ultrasound. The fix: anticoagulants until the clot dissolves.

GROIN AND HIP

Adductor Strain, Groin Pulls That Won't Go Away

An adductor is a muscle that pulls your leg inward to the center of your body. A groin pull is the strain of the adductor muscle that is

QUICK GUIDE: ADDUCTOR STRAIN
Symptoms: Groin pain that does not get better with physical therapy.
How it occurred: Injury in the area that is not in the muscle.
What the doctor may do: Careful history and physical exam, including X-ray, MRI, leg-length examination, gait analysis. See text.
Likely treatment: Depends on diagnosis. For leg length or overpronation, orthotics or orthotic adjustment, and a stretching and strengthening program. For stress fracture or stress syndrome, rest and further treatment which may include Exogen bone stimulator, PRP, physical therapy, and muscle strengthening and stretching.

responsible for pulling your thigh toward the midline of your body. If you are suffering from pain in that area, you may be told that you have an adductor strain or a groin pull. However, muscle strains that don't get better despite therapy are probably not muscle strains. I saw someone in my office recently with this condition. She had a stress fracture of the pubic ramus (the upper part of the pubic bone in the pelvis). Therapy would not help this condition if she continued to exercise; the working of the muscles during exercise would only continue to aggravate the injury. Rest—meaning no impact exercise within this area—for eight weeks would have to be followed to heal this problem.

If you are suffering from what feels like a muscle strain that won't go away, please find a physician who will spend some time with you and be as curious as can be about what is going on and why you got it. Ask this physician for the following:

1. An X-ray of your pelvis and upper femur. If it's negative, you'll need an MRI to see if there is a stress fracture or bone edema (stress syndrome). The MRI can also show in the same film if there is truly a muscle strain present.

2. An assessment of leg length. If you do have a stress fracture, it very likely could be caused by a leg-length discrepancy (see page 179).

3. An assessment for overpronation when you run.

4. If (2) and/or (3) is positive, you will need flexible, full-length orthotics in your shoes to correct things. If leg length is off, the difference should be corrected only by half (that is,

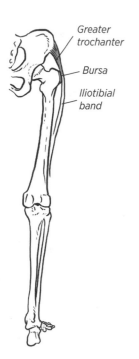

Figure IV.34

Greater trochanteric hip bursitis

if there is a quarter-inch difference, a correction should be made of one-eighth inch); otherwise, the correction will be too great and further discomfort will result.

Greater Trochanteric Hip Bursitis

QUICK GUIDE: GREATER TROCHANTERIC HIP BURSITIS
Symptoms: Pain at outside of hip.
How it occurred: Repetitive motion causing friction on bursa.
What the doctor may do: Palpate area. X-ray, MRI not necessary.
Likely treatment: Cortisone injection. PRP injection if cortisone only brings partial relief. ITB stretches can sometimes relieve and/or prevent condition.

Sometimes iliotibial band syndrome pain (see page 155) that is felt only at the hip may not be ITB syndrome after all. There is a small bursa at the hip that can get irritated, and the resulting condition, greater trochanteric hip bursitis, can be diagnosed only by an experienced physician who knows what to feel for. The good news is a simple cortisone shot or a PRP injection (see page 124) is all that is needed for you to be pain-free within a week.

I am always asked how these injuries occur. The annoying answer is, no one knows. We think a tight ITB can rub this bursa, so stretching the ITB (as recommended on pages 156 and 157) if you are tight is a good idea. That said, I have also seen this in patients with very loose ITBs, so go figure! Just know that if you have it and it is properly diagnosed, the condition is a needle stick away from being gone.

Osteitis Pubis

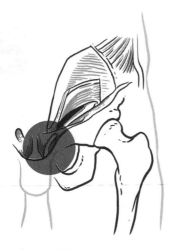

Figure IV.35

Osteitis pubis

It's tempting to assume that every pain in the pubic area is just another run-of-the-mill groin pull like you had last time and that stretching the area before every workout will take care of it. Fortunately or unfortunately, the hip area is a little more complicated than that. And one of the common but frequently undiagnosed ways it can object to hard training is a condition called osteitis pubis,

QUICK GUIDE: OSTEITIS PUBIS

Symptoms: Pain on or around pubic bone.

How it occurred: Inflammation of the bones where two halves of the pelvis meet, often caused by running shoes with insufficient cushion, or a biomechanical flaw at the feet translated upward.

What the doctor may do: Physical exam. Gait analysis. Leg-length measurements. X-ray. MRI.

Likely treatment: Cushioned shoes. Orthotic or orthotic adjustment. NSAIDs. Ice. Stretching exercises and rest. For advanced cases, corticosteroids (2 weeks). Cortisone injection. PRP injection. Physical therapy. Severe (very rare) cases may require surgery to fuse pubic bones.

an irritation of the pubic bone that can imitate a number of other things, like a hernia.

Osteitis pubis is an inflammation of the bones where the two halves of the pelvis meet in the front. By moving up and down and rotating a little, that pelvis joint does its job mechanically by helping you to be more flexible. But nature supplied the pubic symphysis, as the joint is called, with a stingy blood supply and consequently a great ability to become inflamed, rather than healed, after irritation. So while the joint is absorbing the shocks it was meant to take from the rest of the body, it's not really able to deal with them after it gets them.

The classic osteitis pubis victim I see is a runner, male or female, who's been pounding out the miles on hard surfaces in worn shoes that no longer cushion or possibly had too little cushioning to begin with. Men who've had prostate surgery are more vulnerable. In the early stages of this condition, a mild stretching program to loosen all the muscles that attach to and therefore pull on the groin area might have been enough, plus some rest or at least an exercise switch to water running, swimming, or even cycling on smooth roads. But by the time I see most athletes, their futile "groin pull" therapy piled on top of a full training schedule has produced severe pain, with particular tenderness right on the pubic bone. Now it hurts even worse when they stretch, and the softening of the pubic bone from all the irritation is obvious enough to be seen on a common X-ray.

GROIN & HIP

By the time the inflammation has gone this far, it's going to take some medication to reverse. Two weeks on corticosteroids are usually enough to erase the symptoms, but you can be on limited or alternate exercise for as much as two months. A cortisone shot or PRP (see page 124) and physical therapy are sometimes needed to help relieve that inflammation. Ignoring osteitis pubis will not make it go away. In fact if it's untreated long enough, the condition becomes chronic, and the only choice left is surgery to actually fuse the pubic bone so that it no longer moves.

BACK

It has been said that everyone, at some point, will have some back pain. The good news for runners, walkers, and cyclists is that these endurance sports do not cause structural damage to the back. Lifting sports and heredity are the primary causes of structural back problems.

However, it is also true that running, jogging, and sprinting are more stressful on your back than, say, walking. Running transmits a lot of jarring and impact to the spine and back muscles, and these forces are not always well tolerated by spines susceptible to back pain. The Basic 8 exercises presented here will go a long way toward eliminating the aches and pains that backs may suffer from regular exercise.

Keep in mind, too, that the most common cause of back pain in runners is not a vulnerable spine at all, but the result of a leg-length discrepancy that causes low-back muscular strain (see page 179 in this section for more detail on leg-length problems). Take a longer leg and a shorter leg out for a run, and you can imagine the side-to-side tug-of-war going on at your hip and within your back muscles. No back exercises can fully prepare you for that or cure you of the resultant pain. The good news is that leg-length differences can be easily corrected with orthotic devices that slip into your shoes.

It is not the intention of this short discussion to be a full description of the causes and treatments of back pain because there are way too many to discuss here. The most important thing for runners to know is that there are more muscles and ligaments within the back than anywhere else in the body, so we need to prepare those muscles with specific exercises so that they don't get strained or pulled during a run. That's why the Basic 8 include pelvic stabilization exercises and stretches of the hamstrings and quadriceps in addition to strengthening exercises for the quadriceps and hamstrings that power so much of a runner's movement.

Sciatica

QUICK GUIDE: SCIATICA

Symptoms: Low back pain radiating down the leg.

How it occurred: Sciatica is only a symptom of other conditions.

What the doctor may do: Accurate diagnosis to pinpoint the actual condition and cure.

Likely treatment: Depends on cause.

Tell me if you'd settle for this: You hobble from the tennis court into your doctor's office after a clumsy off-kilter lunge blew up your ankle like a puffy softball. Ow! Dr. What-Have-We-Here looks thoughtful. He palpates the ankle (medical talk for "feels carefully"), pulls and twists it to test ligament strength. Next, he taps on the bone to see whether it's tender. Grave looks, off you go to X-ray, and when the film comes back, Dr. W. tosses it up on the light box and knits his brows. "Yes, yes," he concludes, rubbing his chin and straightening up. "It's quite apparent. What you have here is called a swollen ankle."

Nonsense? Certainly. But not much different from a diagnosis of "sciatica" whenever back pain is presented, which is something that athletes run into time and again when they seek help with low back pain radiating down the leg. The most sophisticated medical consumers I know, runners are nevertheless still getting and buying one of the big, bogus diagnoses of all time: sciatica. Bogus because it somehow makes you feel good without actually revealing a thing about what's wrong. But it's a symptom, not a diagnosis!

Everyone deserves better, as I say over and over in my practice. Too long have we thought of spines, including the spine of the athlete, as stiff columns of bony structures from which radiate the

BACK

most mysterious of pains. But spines are, instead, highly flexible. As I always say, you just have to ask the right questions and pursue the search until you get the real answer.

Why, then, do some physicians simply stick sciatica onto so many athletes like a diagnostic Post-it, then give them a couple of generic exercises and send them away? Why did sciatica become the catchall term the doctors give as a diagnosis over and over? Because, frankly, a lot of back patients don't ever improve. They return repeatedly with the same complaint, and the doctor eventually begins to wonder whether they even *want* to recover, overlooking the fact that it could be the treatment that's not hitting the target. A more refined answer takes additional time and effort, whereas the diagnosis of sciatica is a simple way of letting the patient walk out of the office happy with an answer. Beyond that, sciatica is a reimbursable diagnosis code, so no complaints from either side for the time being.

The sciatic nerve runs down your leg; it originates higher up as nerves feed into each other like so many streams and tributaries and eventually emerge from between the vertebrae of the spinal column as a single nerve of many parts. The nerves weave themselves together somewhere around your butt, and the sciatic nerve goes down your leg and spreads out again to all parts of the leg.

Trouble is, that tingling or painful sensation going down or in your leg could be caused by any number of things happening to any number of nerves way upstream. Degenerative disc disease, which we all get as the little padded discs between the vertebrae gradually dry out and lose their cushioning as we age, can let a vertebra settle onto a nerve and irritate or pinch it. A facet joint at the back of a vertebra can get out of alignment. A strained back muscle might go into spasm and painfully squeeze a nearby nerve or nerve sheath. Even running with a leg-length discrepancy, the most common back pain culprit of all among my patients, can cause sciatica.

The list goes on and on, but fortunately these are not unfathomable mysteries. They can and will be found by someone determined to get to the bottom of a patient's back pain because we now have the

Laying the Foundation for a Healthy Back

Strong abdominal muscles, supple hip flexors, and firm butt muscles help make a runner's back flexible and sound. There are inescapable demands every one of us makes every day on the spine's support system, and if you want your back to move easily, effectively, powerfully, and painlessly, step one is to target the basic muscle systems, the key "marionette strings" if you will, and get to work making them limber and strong. That's just what the Basic 8 exercises here will accomplish. Plan to do all eight exercises five times a week, with two days off. Think of them as the foundation for a strong runner's body!

Figure IV.36

Pelvic tilt

Lying on your back with your knees flexed, tighten your stomach and flatten your back to the floor by rolling your pelvis down. Hold for 10 seconds. Relax. Repeat four more times, with a 5-second rest after each pelvic tilt. One set equals five repeats.

Figure IV.37

Double knee to chest

Lying on your back with your hands behind your knees, pull both knees to your chest until a comfortable stretch is felt in your lower back and buttocks. Keep your back relaxed. Hold for 10 seconds. Relax. Rest for 5 seconds with your legs straightened and resting on the ground. Then repeat four more times for a total of five repetitions. One set equals five repeats.

Figure IV.38

Trunk flex

While on your hands and knees, push your chest toward the floor, reaching forward as far as possible. Hold for 10 seconds. Relax. Repeat four more times for a total of five, with a 5-second rest after each repetition. One set equals five repeats.

continues

Laying the Foundation for a Healthy Back, continued

Figure IV.39

The cat

While on your hands and knees, tuck your chin and tighten your stomach while arching your back. Hold for 10 seconds. Relax. Repeat four more times for a total of five, with a 5-second rest between repetitions. One set equals five repeats.

Figure IV.40

Partial sit-up

Lie on your back with your knees flexed. Fold your arms across your chest, and tilt your pelvis to flatten your back against the floor. Then raise your head and shoulders from the floor, but do not sit up all the way. Hold for 10 seconds, and then lower yourself back to the floor. Repeat. One set equals 25 repeats with a 3-second rest between repetitions. As you become more comfortable with this exercise, you can increase the number of partial sit-ups to whatever number you can do.

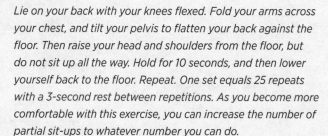

Figure IV.41

Hip extension

Lying on your stomach with a pillow for support, lift your left leg 10 inches from the floor, keeping your knee locked. Hold for 10 seconds. Lower your leg. Then repeat with right leg to complete a set. Repeat the set four more times for a total of five, with a 5-second rest between repetitions.

diagnostic tools to do that. And each cause has a specific treatment. General physical therapy, often recommended for sciatica, is like taking a shotgun and blasting away at a barn; but with an accurate diagnosis the therapy can take precise aim at the bull's-eye and get you running again, pain-free!

To be fair, it wasn't always possible to be this accurate. Just as we once had to settle for "internal derangement of the knee" as a diagnosis before arthrograms let us inject dye into joints and X-ray the results, before MRIs and other diagnostic tools let us pinpoint anterior cruciate ligament tears and medial collateral ligament tears and other

Figure IV.42

Quad stretch

While standing near a table or chair for support, pull your right heel toward your butt until you can feel the stretch in the front of your thigh. Hold for 10 seconds. Lower your leg. Then repeat with left heel to complete a set. Repeat the set four more times for a total of five, with a 5-second rest between repetitions.

Figure IV.43

Standing hamstring stretch

While standing, place your right foot on a stool or low bench. While keeping your back straight, slowly lean forward until you feel the stretch in the back of your thigh. Hold for 10 seconds. Repeat with left leg to complete one set. Repeat the set four more times for a total of five, with a 5-second rest between repetitions.

knee joint problems that we can now treat specifically and effectively, sciatica was once the best we could do with the mysterious back.

But the mystery's gone now. If "sciatica" is as far as you can get with your physician, consult someone else. You don't want a Post-it. You want a probe. Then you can research the best way to treat your condition and run pain-free!

Piriformis Syndrome

Piriformis syndrome is—figuratively and literally—a pain in the butt, one that does an excellent imitation of the catchall ailment called

BACK

> **QUICK GUIDE: PIRIFORMIS SYNDROME**
>
> **Symptoms:** Pain in midbutt, which can radiate upward toward the back and down the leg with sciatica symptoms.
>
> **How it occurred:** Forced toe-out (like a ballet step) while running (as if trying to miss a puddle).
>
> **What the doctor may do:** Complete history. Physical exam (doctor should be able to feel muscle spasm in middle of butt). Gait analysis. Injury will not show up on X-ray or MRI. Doctors tend to order an MRI to rule out disc herniation. In my view, an MRI should be a confirmation, not a fishing expedition.
>
> **Likely treatment:** Physical therapy. Orthotic or orthotic adjustment. Electronic muscle stimulation. Cortisone injection. PRP injection.

sciatica. This pain can also show up in the lowermost portion of the back, which is why I've included it in this section. Therapy is possible but tricky. Don't try to diagnose and treat this one yourself.

Not long ago, for example, Paul, a 45-year-old patient of mine, came to me with what he described as a dull ache in the middle of one buttock. It hurt him to run, and the pain was especially sharp as he was going up hills or even walking up stairs. A string of doctors had pegged it as everything from a deteriorated spinal disc to that classic medical non sequitur, low back pain. None apparently suspected the piriformis, one of the muscles deep in the rear of the pelvis that helps turn your leg outward and that runs alongside, and occasionally surrounds, the sciatic nerve. Like any muscle, it can be overused and go into spasm, something that can also be triggered by tight hamstrings, prolonged sitting, or anything that twists the area. When that happens—and especially when the sciatic nerve becomes involved—the pain is dull, constant, and, it often seems, permanent.

Diagnosis is not difficult for anyone who has seen the condition before. One or two simple exercises with the patient on a table can pinpoint it, and trained fingers can actually feel down to and sense the spasming muscle. But diagnosis is only the start of treatment, and therapy is far from simple, news that is always a big disappointment to experienced athletes who are

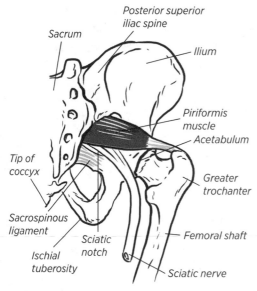

Figure IV.44A

Piriformis muscle location

accustomed to being sent home with a list of simple stretching and strengthening exercises and a follow-up appointment.

Paul, for example, listened to me for 20 minutes while I explained why he had to do exactly as I said. Yes, there would be stretches, but they would have to be done with the guidance of a physical therapist. Beyond that, because the muscle is so deep and the spasm so hard to break, we would also need to gang up other available therapies, including cortisone or PRP shots (see page 124); a specialized technique called transverse frictional massage in which the massage is applied opposite the alignment of the muscle and tendon fibers; electrogalvanic stimulation of the tissues, where an electric current is applied to break up the pain messages in the nerves; ice; and ultrasound. Paul was supposed to follow up with me every four weeks during his physical therapy.

I heard from him nine months later when he called to tell me how disappointed he had been with my care. Why? Because he still hurt. Of course, it turns out that once he knew what was wrong with him, he'd decided to skip all that therapy stuff, get some piriformis stretches out of a book (they're easy to find), and get to work on his own.

A condition that's commonly not correctly diagnosed in the first place, that requires otherwise intelligent athletes to follow orders like robots, and that's all but impervious to anything but the full galaxy of therapies is as close as one can come to a sports medicine physician's nightmare. But if you do what you're told, it needn't be your nightmare, too.

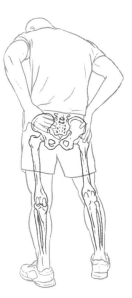

Figure IV.44B

Piriformis syndrome, full-body view

Sacroiliac Joint

QUICK GUIDE: SACROILIAC JOINT

Symptoms: Low back pain, thigh pain, pain in butt.

How it occurred: Lack of mobility in joint.

What the doctor may do: Physical exam. Gait analysis. Leg length measurement. X-ray. CT scan. MRI.

Likely treatment: Physical therapy. Orthotics or orthotic adjustment. Lower extremity stretching program. Core strengthening program. Heel lift if needed at one-half leg length discrepancy. Corticosteroid injection. PRP injection.

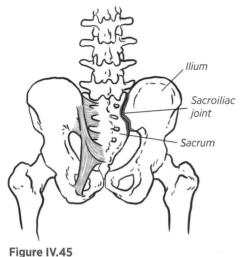

Figure IV.45

Sacroiliac joint

Ilium

Sacroiliac joint

Sacrum

The sacroiliac (SI) joint was a very popular diagnosis for all sorts of leg and back pain 20 years ago, and yet for some reason it is forgotten or overlooked by many physicians nowadays. Let's explore the SI area for a moment so that we all *re*-remember how important this joint is to pain-free living.

The sacroiliac joint is one of two joints in your pelvis that connect the tailbone (the sacrum) and the large pelvic bone (the ilium). The sacroiliac joint connects the spine to the pelvis and therefore to the entire lower half of the skeleton. As with all true joints, there is articular cartilage on both sides of the sacroiliac joint surfaces. Unlike most other joints, the SI joint is not designed for much motion. In fact, it is common for the sacroiliac joint to actually lock up.

The sacroiliac joint usually moves only about two to four millimeters during weight-bearing and forward flexion. This small amount of motion occurring in the joint is a gliding type of motion as opposed to the hinge type of motion of the knee or the ball-and-socket motion of the shoulder. The SI joint's main function is to provide shock absorption for the spine, and it does so through this gliding type of movement.

Doctors find SI problems difficult to diagnose because there is a confusing pattern of back pain and pelvic pain that mimic each other. You may have no symptoms other than the fact that your runner's knee (page 150) is not responding to treatment. Symptoms may include any or all of the following:

- Low back pain
- Thigh pain, particularly lateral thigh
- Butt pain, mimicking Piriformis syndrome
- Sciaticlike pain
- Difficulty sitting in one place for too long due to pain in lower back

As with everything else, diagnosis is simple when the practitioner knows what to look for:

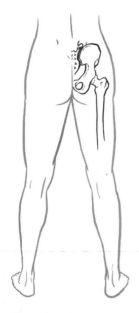

Figure IV.46

Sacroiliac pain location

Normal motion: Facing away from the examiner, with his or her thumbs on the SI joints, you will be asked to raise one leg at a time as if you were marching. A trained examiner will be able to see whether normal motion is occurring or if the joint has locked down.

Gaenslen's test: The examiner will have you lie on a table with both legs brought up to your chest. You will then shift to the side of the table so that one butt cheek is over the edge. The unsupported leg drops over the edge, and the supported leg is flexed. In this position, SI joint problems will cause pain because of stress to the joint.

Patrick's test: The leg is flexed at the knee and brought up to the opposite knee. Then the flexed knee is pressed on to test. Pain at the SI joint is indicative of the problem.

X-rays and a CT scan (also called a "CAT" scan; they're the same thing) may be needed if the cause of the problem is arthritic changes.

If an SI issue is your problem, treatment may range from physical therapy with a therapist who works well with your sports physician to mobilize and/or strengthen the joint, orthotics to balance your musculature, and a corticosteroid injection or PRP injections (see page 124) into the joint to decrease inflammation as you work in therapy. Chiropractic manipulation may or may not be appropriate depending on the anatomy of the joint; discuss with your physician before trying this.

But understanding this oft-overlooked area and addressing it, even if you have runner's knee as well, will get you back on the road faster than ignoring it.

Leg-Length Discrepancy

QUICK GUIDE: LEG-LENGTH DISCREPANCY
Symptoms: Low back pain.
How it occurred: Physical conformation, uneven shoe wear, muscle strain.
What the doctor may do: Physical exam. Measurement of leg length with a tape measure or standing pelvis X-ray. Gait analysis. Examination of running and work shoes.
Likely treatment: Orthotic lift in shoe for short leg (see text for amount of lift). New running shoes if cause is uneven shoe wear.

As you know, I truly understand that though it's good medicine to rule out all serious possibilities when treating an injury, finding out what an illness is *not* is only half the battle. This credo applies as much to back pain as to other complaints, so you can imagine how an athlete I saw recently must have felt after he'd laid out over $5,000 in doctors' fees and about four times that in tests before I ever saw him, and I had to break the news that his problem was something simple he'd been doing to himself all along.

To be honest, back pain caused by leg-length discrepancy can be extremely easy to miss, and that is what happened in Mike's case. When he walked into my office, he looked like the classic runner with low back pain. He was in his late 40s, working out regularly but stretching irregularly, and he was vaguely aware that hamstrings grow tighter with age and can make older athletes vulnerable to a stiff and achy lower back. Mike worked religiously to stretch and strengthen his hamstrings. But his exercise regimen had done no good.

So he'd made up his mind to face "the truth"—he was sure he was in for some kind of surgery. However, the MRI his first physician ordered had turned up nothing. Neither had a CT scan. Nor had X-rays, flexion-extension X-rays, and a CT myelogram to check for disc trouble. (Flexion-extension X-rays are X-rays taken with the area fully extended and then fully flexed; a CT myelogram uses a dye injected into the joint to help make the area more visible on the scan.) Every one of the several doctors he'd been to since then had given him the most plausible diagnosis: He probably had a pulled or strained muscle that needed stretching and strengthening. After $10,000 in electronic imaging, he was back where he started.

Here we go again, I thought. This guy never bothered to tell his doctors that he ran 40 miles a week. No wonder they had him tested for everything else in the book. But if this wasn't a classic leg-length discrepancy case, I don't know an orthotic from an Ace bandage. After all, it doesn't take much to throw your gait off and make the longer leg work harder, which is usually the side where the pain is more pronounced. A difference as meager as a quarter inch will do it.

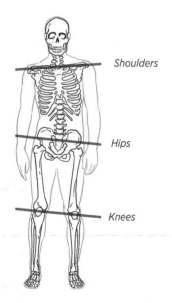

Figure IV.47

Leg-length discrepancy

Shoulders

Hips

Knees

When Leg-Length Discrepancy Is Not in Your Legs

Not every leg-length problem among runners is in the legs. Sometimes it's in the runner's shoes. Let me explain.

Another running patient, Dave, appeared in my office some time ago with lower back symptoms and a treatment history almost identical to Mike's. I listened to his history of failed diagnoses and then sized him up with my trusty tape measure (though leg-length differences can be measured extremely finely with a standing pelvic X-ray, a well-managed tape measure can usually tell us all we need to know), and the astonishing news this tape measure was telling me was that Dave was actually symmetrical. His legs were the same length. Precisely. Despite all the incriminating evidence to the contrary, including the cello-string-tight back muscles on the side of what should have been his longer leg, his legs weren't the problem. So where could this guy be getting his back trouble from anyway?

Right at the end of his legs. Turns out that Dave had more than a fondness for his running shoes. He had a relationship with them, wearing them the way some of us wear a favorite sweater for years and years. Oh, he knew about the 500-mile cutoff, after which most shoes should be retired because they are too beaten up to do much good anymore. But these were his "lucky trainers." What would he do without them?

Stop his back pain, that's what. After what he conservatively guessed was 1,200 miles of punishment, Dave's shoes were understandably badly broken down. But it was how they had broken down that mattered: unevenly. Thanks to who knows what—a manufacturing peculiarity, a quirk in Dave's gait, maybe even the angle of the roads he'd run on—one shoe was about a quarter inch lower than the other. Shorter legs or shorter shoes, turns out his body didn't discriminate. Very probably, most wouldn't.

So I had to advise Dave to spend just a little more, about $100 or so for some new footwear. "Lose the old shoes and you'll lose the pain," I promised. And he did.

My suggestion to everyone: Go to your sports doctor, and don't give up or allow a nonanswer. Be a persistent, educated consumer. And always take your running shoes with you to the exam. A good sports doc will always ask to look at them!

The remedy for Mike, and anyone else with this problem, is simple: Put a small lift in the other shoe. Usually about half the size of the spread is enough, so a quarter-inch difference in leg length would generally be successfully treated with an eighth-inch lift.

HEAD

Concussion

QUICK GUIDE: CONCUSSION

Symptoms: Headache, dizziness, loss of consciousness, amnesia, nausea, vomiting, seizure.

How it occurred: Blow to the head through falling or through running into something.

What the doctor may do: Complete neurological exam. CT scan of head. MRI.

Likely treatment: Clearance from physician before resuming activity.

When someone hits his or her head, a prompt and proper evaluation is important. Brain injury must be recognized and treated seriously.

Concussion comes from the Latin *concutera*, which means "to shake violently." The brain is suspended in fluid within the skull, and traumatic brain injury can occur from the brain hitting the side walls of the skull. When this happens, the brain can be merely bruised (still not good), or it can develop life-threatening bleeds. Physicians grade concussions on a scale from slight conditions (where only dizziness occurs) to postunconscious states; anything within this continuum can lead to a postconcussive syndrome of headaches, dizziness, and further damage in the event of a second concussion on top of the first.

It is my best recommendation that if an athlete experiences a head injury and has any one or more of the following symptoms, the athlete should not be moved until emergency medical technicians arrive to do so. The injured party should be transported to a hospital by ambulance and evaluated by an emergency room physician. To avoid any complications from a possible neck injury, this protocol, which may seem overcautious, is very important if the injury is from a fall where the head has taken a blow. Here is a list of the indicative symptoms:

- Dizziness
- Headache
- Loss of consciousness

- Pre- or postfall amnesia
- Nausea
- Vomiting
- Seizure

After evaluation and diagnosis of a concussion, it may take three weeks or more for you to become "normal" again. A clearance from an examining physician permitting participation in sports activities is important before you resume your routine. Your doctor wants to make absolutely sure that you exhibit no signs of postconcussive syndrome, which is essential for long-term health.

HEAD

PART V
SUDDEN DEATH AND RUNNING

Sudden Death and Running

Five Steps to Prevention

The International Marathon Medical Directors Association was founded in 1982 by the directors of the London, Madrid, and New York City marathons with the goal of sharing knowledge about medical issues among the people we treat and oversee at races. The association has since grown to include marathon medical directors from all five continents who study the health of long-distance runners, promote knowledge of the best methods in prevention and treatment of injuries, and offer guidelines that may provide standardization in the medical support of marathon races throughout the world. The IMMDA is affiliated with the Association of International Marathons and Distance Races and has provided guidelines in the medical management of marathons covering the topics of heat stress, cardiac risks, running injury prevention, and many other important subjects.

One of the most critical topics under discussion and study is sudden cardiac death (death from the heart stopping) in marathons. Specifically, we've been trying to identify why we have been seeing these deaths within 1 mile of the finish. As race medical directors, we are all stationing paramedic units at that very section—from 1 mile before the finish to the finish line itself—and are as amazed as anyone at how we can predict the place where runners go down.

There are two prevailing theories about sudden death in healthy patients doing an endurance event. One theory is that a caffeine load of more than 200 mg (more than two normal-sized cups of coffee) has caused sufficiently decreased blood flow to the point where the heart's rhythm is disrupted (this type of sudden death is known as fatal cardiac arrhythmia; "arrhythmia" is a change in the rhythm of the heartbeat). The other theory is that the release of muscle by-products during the event causes a small plaque—basically, a lesion in an artery—to activate platelets, which in turn form a small clot in a coronary artery. There are two coronary arteries; their job is to supply blood to the heart itself. When a clot forms in one of them, blood flow to the heart is reduced, and fatal arrhythmia often follows. In both cases, limiting caffeine and taking a baby aspirin daily should eliminate these possibilities.

The 1-mile mark is an interesting component of this sudden death syndrome for marathon runners. Certainly, it seems to be a place where participants finally know that they will finish or where they can see the finish line and therefore push themselves to a hard sprint finish. This adrenaline rush, we theorize, might push the electrical system of the heart to an arrhythmia if the heart muscle is ischemic by one of the two mechanisms just described or if the participant has underlying heart disease. Not pushing yourself that last mile and instead taking it as you have the last few miles might make participating safer. So would encouraging announcers not to goad runners by saying things like "If you can hear my voice, you can break four hours!"

I am looking forward to the time when our IMMDA group will be outlining a worldwide study on sudden death in our sport. As of now we have only some small evidence from a few studies and a lot of anecdotal evidence and theory. Our study should put more science into our recommendation.

In the meantime, we continue to advise the following:

1. Be sure to have a yearly physical exam and tell the examiner exactly what you are training for and how. Indicate your training pace and your expected finishing time. All of that information may change the tests and the approach to the examination.

2. If you develop new chest pain or more shortness of breath than usual during training or during a race, STOP and seek medical attention immediately.

3. Ask your doctor about taking a baby aspirin (81 mg) daily or—at the very least—before any long run or race. If you have no contraindications, do it. You can take the pill at any time in the morning before your run.

4. Limit your caffeine intake on the day of a long run or race (see the next section for a discussion of the possible role of caffeine). Less than 200 mg of caffeine on race day and training days (about 2 regular-size cups of coffee; note that one 16 oz Starbucks Grande has about 330 mg!) seems to be the number we're talking about.

5. Finally, run the last mile of the race like the previous miles, without a fast sprint.

These recommendations make sense to me and my fellow marathon medical directors. When our patients ask, "How can I prevent my being the next one?" our advice—right after urging them to get a comprehensive physical—consists of the steps just listed. I hope you follow this advice as well, in collaboration with your physician.

The Case Against Caffeine

Not long ago discussion among physicians who are members of the IMMDA described the following recent cases of successful resuscitations at different races around the world:

-   A 33-year-old male running a half-marathon dropped at the 12-mile mark, at 3:10 into his race. The morning of the race, he had drunk two energy drinks and a Starbucks Grande coffee and had used two caffeinated gels. An examination revealed a small lesion (less than 20 percent) but otherwise clean coronary arteries.

-   A 42-year-old woman running a marathon dropped at the 24.5-mile mark, 4:10 into her run. She had drunk two large coffees and had had three caffeinated gels. Her examination also showed clean coronaries.

- A 26-year-old male running a marathon dropped at the 25.5-mile mark, 3:25 into his run. He had taken two caffeine pills plus coffee the morning of the race and also had clean arteries.

More cases were discussed. We also noted that the press always covers the deaths at these events, not the many more numerous successful resuscitations that are performed. But the press is missing the story: It is with the successful resuscitations that we can interview the patients and find out what they did that might have contributed to their collapse.

So is caffeine definitely the culprit in these deaths? As I said, we just don't know. But here are some preliminary thoughts:

- Over the past several years, consumption of caffeine has taken off, especially among younger people. Whereas we once got caffeine mainly from our morning coffee, today we have espresso shots in that coffee, caffeine-loaded drinks like Red Bull and RockStar, even caffeine-laced energy gels. And at least one study has shown that 200 mg of caffeine decreases coronary blood flow during a marathon. Could high doses of caffeine be enough to set off a fatal arrhythmia?
- Dr. Arthur Siegel, director of internal medicine at McLean Hospital in Belmont, Massachusetts, and a medical volunteer for the Boston Marathon, has reported that platelet activation from plaque due to muscle breakdown from marathon running may be a cause of a microischemic event causing a fatal arrhythmia not seen on autopsy.

Others propose that there is another underlying problem that has not, as yet, been identified. IMMDA is putting together a research project to examine this question as well as a statistical study of how many people actually are successfully resuscitated per number entered. (We know that statistically 1 in 50,000 marathoners dies worldwide per year.) In the meantime, I recommend that you limit your consumption of caffeine to 200 mg per day on days of a long run or a race of 10K or longer. To help you monitor your caffeine consumption, I've included a table of caffeine content in soft drinks,

How Much Caffeine Is in That Drink?

SOFT DRINKS

According to the Center for Science in the Public Interest, the following is the caffeine content in milligrams per 12-ounce can:

SOFT DRINK	CAFFEINE (MILLIGRAMS)
7UP	0
Canada Dry Cola	30.0
Canada Dry Diet Cola	1.2
Coca-Cola Classic	35.0
Coca-Cola Zero	35.0
Diet Coke	45.6
Diet Rite	36.0
Dr. Pepper	39.6
Jolt	71.2
Kick Citrus	54.0 (36 mg per 8 oz can)
Mello Yellow	52.8
Mountain Dew	55.0 (no caffeine in Canada)
Mountain Dew, Diet	55.0
Mr. Pibb	40.8
Mr. Pibb, sugar-free	58.8
OK Soda	40.5
Pepsi Cola	37.2
Pepsi Cola, Diet	35.4
RC Cola	36.0
RC Cola, Diet	36.0
Shasta Cola	44.4
Shasta Cherry Cola	44.4
Shasta Diet Cola	44.4
Snapple Lemon Tea, 16 oz	42.0
Sprite	0
Surge	51.0
Tab	46.8

continues

How Much Caffeine Is in That Drink?, continued

COFFEE, TEA

The American Beverage Association provides the following data on caffeine content in milligrams for 8-ounce drinks:

Coffee, drip	104–192
Tea, brewed	20–90
Iced tea	9–50

OTHER SOURCES OF CAFFEINE

Content in milligrams:

Mate, 8 oz	25–150
Hot cocoa, 8 oz	3–32
Milk chocolate, 1 oz	1–15
Dark chocolate, 1 oz	5–35
Vivarin tablet	200
Generic stay-awake pill	100
Cold relief tablet with caffeine	30

coffee drinks, and other forms. Add up the caffeine you ingest every day; you may be surprised to see that it is much more than 200 mg!

When Trouble Strikes

As you may know, I am the medical director for numerous marathons, and each of these marathons has a large medical team. Our safety record, in my mind, is based not only on the presence and efficacy of these medical teams, which are all oriented to running medicine, but also on our development of a strategy of rapid response to a "runner down." Our response team consists of a central Medical Control station and a series of smaller satellite medical stations placed every mile along the course. In addition, each medical station then sends a spotter one-half mile down the road toward the next station so that we effectively have eyes on the course every half-mile. The spotters have my phone number at Medical Control so that if someone needs assistance, I can get an ambulance or medical person to him or her rapidly.

Medical Control is a concept that more and more marathons are now using. Some call this a "unified command center" because all agencies from the city send a representative and we work together. In this tent are phones that the medical captains at each satellite station can call in to. We also have ambulance control sited here, with a big map of the course on which we track and update the positions and movements of the ambulances. All of the event staff and coaches are given Medical Control's phone numbers to get an ambulance dispatched as quickly as possible. Having dedicated numbers is important because 911 calls are received by the city. When a 911 call is made concerning the event, the call is redirected to our control center, but it is faster to call the Medical Control number first, reserving 911 as a backup in case the call to Medical Control does not go through.

I believe every medical director would welcome participants of the race serving as spotters. More eyes on the course is obviously better. If you are interested in volunteering your help, ask race management for the Medical Control telephone number. Then if you come upon someone needing assistance, you will be ready to lend a hand.

Should you come across someone who needs medical attention, please follow the outline here. In this way, you will make a difference for a downed runner in your race!

1. First look around for a medical team member. Team members usually wear red T-shirts. If you see one, please get one of these people and let him or her handle the situation.

2. *Do not move the patient.* He or she may have fallen and have a hurt neck.

3. If you do not see someone with a red T-shirt, follow these guidelines:
   - Do not call 911 first. Instead, call Medical Control. If you can't get through, then call 911. Take a deep breath because everyone naturally gets nervous in these situations.

- State exactly where you are. Give us an address, exact street corner, or specific location along the course or within the start or finish area if possible. "By a tree" is not enough information for us to provide immediate assistance.
- Say you are a volunteer with a patient needing assistance.
- Tell Medical Control whether the patient is conscious or unconscious, breathing or not breathing.
- Be able to describe what the person looks like and what he or she is wearing.
- If the injured party is a participant, please also give us the race number.

4. Do not hang up until you are told to. Depending on the situation, we may give you further instructions. The worst thing to hear at my end is "I got a runner down" and then a click indicating the caller hung up!

- Give us your cell phone number. If you get disconnected or we need additional information to locate the patient, we will call you back.
- Stay with the patient until help arrives. Look for the ambulance or med team member, and wave your hands so that help can find you.

If you are considering helping out, it would be a good idea for you to take a cardiopulmonary resuscitation (CPR) course given by your local Red Cross or American Heart Association. Do not attempt CPR if you haven't taken a course. Proper placement of hands and depth of compression are important and can't be learned by watching a TV show. I have seen punctured lungs and pericardium from fractured ribs due to badly performed CPR. Also, I'd recommend that if you took a CPR course some years ago, it would be worthwhile to take a refresher course; recommendations may have changed over the years, and your course instructor will have the most recent advice and approved protocol to share. If you do not know CPR but you are with someone who does and who asks for your help, do not hesitate as she or he should be able to lead you through what you can do safely.

If you see a downed runner while on a training run, have no medical knowledge, and do not know CPR, you can still be of great help:

1. First dial 911. If you are with someone, have that person dial 911 while you tend to the downed runner. Make sure you or your friend has an accurate description of where you are.

2. Assess whether the patient is conscious. Yell, "Are you OK?" and gently tap his or her shoulder. If there is no response, assume that the person is unconscious.

3. At this point, do not roll the patient onto his or her back; he or she may have an injured neck from the fall to the ground.

4. Next, assess for breathing. Is the chest rising or falling? Put your ear up to the mouth and listen. If you are carrying a mirror (some women actually carry a compact when they run!), put the mirror by the nose and mouth, and look for fogging of the mirror.

5. If the patient is breathing, your next step is to observe and wait with the patient, not moving him or her until the ambulance arrives. Be sure to wave your hands as the vehicle approaches so that ambulance personnel can see where you are.

6. If the patient is not breathing, you need to do more. If the person is facedown, gently roll him or her onto the back, supporting the head and neck in line in case there is a fracture. Gently place your fist under the neck so as to raise the chin and open the airway. Place your mouth over the patient's mouth, have a good seal, and blow in until you see the chest rise. Then take your mouth off, allow the patient's chest to fall as the breath comes out, and then reseal your mouth and do a second breath.

7. Now, take your index finger and middle finger (not your thumb because it has a pulse in it) and check the side of the neck for a pulse (feel your own neck so that you know where to place your fingers). If you can't feel a pulse, chest compressions are necessary.

8. Although I would rather you had a CPR course to teach you to do this, something is better than nothing. Place your

midsternum (the place on the chest where the lower ribs meet), and do 100 compressions a minute. The 2010 American Heart Association guidelines say you do not need to give breaths; just keep doing compressions until help arrives.

9. If the patient vomits, carefully roll the patient to the side, keeping the neck in line until clear of vomitus; then recheck breathing and pulse and resume compressions.

10. If the patient is seizing, watch until it finishes; seizures are usually self-limiting. After the seizure stops, check the person again for breathing. Keeping the patient's airway open until help arrives is always a good thing.

I believe everyone should know CPR. There is a free Internet course you can do in no time at all to put your knowledge base way ahead of that of your peers. Please go to www.firstaidweb.com/index .php to get more information.

Postscript: Enjoy the Ride

You now have all the tools you'll need to enjoy your marathon, half-marathon, 10K, or 5K experience, whether this race is your first one or your next one. My accumulated wisdom of watching, talking to, and treating thousands of marathon finishers from the very front to the very back of the pack is in your hands. And if you've read this far, it's now in your head, too. So have the confidence you deserve, and you'll find that the party weekend you hope for will turn out to be just that—a good run and a lot of fun.

Runners, as you probably know by now, love nothing more than sharing advice and opinions. Every runner has his or her own favorite story about getting hurt or getting better or knocking huge chunks of time off a personal best with exactly three swallows of de-fizzed Coke at the 18-mile mark. Some ideas are solid; others fall into the category of "lucky charms." Use this book whenever you get confused about which is which. Nothing here is lore or superstition—it's all sound medicine. Running Doc is on your bookshelf. Use me. Work with me as my patients do. Like those thousands of smiling folks having their 26.2-mile street party, I promise you will love the experience.

Enjoy the ride.

Appendix A

IMMDA'S HEALTH RECOMMENDATIONS FOR RUNNERS AND WALKERS

*Writing committee: Lewis G. Maharam, MD, FACSM (chair),
Arthur Siegel, MD, Stephen Siegel, MD, Bruce Adams, MD,
Pedro Pujol, MD, FACSM, and
Paulo Alfonso Lourega de Menezes, MD*

Approved by IMMDA Body, March 20, 2010
Barcelona, Spain

As Medical Directors (IMMDA: International Marathon Medical Directors Association) of the world's largest marathons and endurance events, it is our desire to educate and ensure that our participants remain healthy and perform well. With increased numbers of participants of both marathons and half marathons throughout the world, and increased attention to Sudden Death by the media and lay public, we have focused our efforts to understanding this phenomena and how it can be prevented.

Rationale

Marathon and half-marathon participation is an extreme endurance sport with intrinsic risks inherent in understanding and respecting these distances. Current theory behind Sudden Death in these athletes, based on preliminary research and observations include:

Underlying Conditions not previously found in the athlete.

There is evidence that exercise can increase the risk of cardiac events, including heart attack and death. The risk is reduced by regular exercise. Attempts to exceed the intensity or duration of an established level of exercise may induce compensatory mechanisms that are deleterious.

Endurance exercise releases muscle enzymes which may activate platelets and produce a thrombus and cardiac ischemia.

There are studies that indicate an increased risk associated with increased caffeine consumption above 200 mg during endurance exercise.

Hyponatremia is a preventable condition if participants drink [a] sports drink or its equivalent for thirst, don't take nonsteroidal anti-inflammatories (NSAIDs) during running, and consume salt.

Sprinting the last mile may increase adrenaline and take a susceptible myocardium into an abnormal rhythm.

Recommendations

In an attempt to reduce the risks of Sudden Death, IMMDA has developed the following guidelines. We have attempted to use the best available scientific research to support these guidelines with the understanding that we are conducting new research worldwide and may modify these recommendations in the future.

1. Participants should not only be sufficiently trained, but equally important, they should have a goal and corresponding race plan that is appropriate for that level of training and fitness. If not, do not attempt the distance.

2. Have a yearly physical examination being sure to discuss your exercise plans, goals and intensity at that visit.

3. Consume one baby aspirin (81 mg) on the morning of a long run/walk of 10K or more if there is no medical contraindication.

4. Consume less than 200 mg caffeine before and during a 10K or more.

5. Only drink a sports drink or its equivalent during a workout of 10K or more.

6. Drink for thirst.

7. Do not consume an NSAID during a run or walk of 10K or more.

8. Consume salt (if no medical contraindication) during a 10K or more.

9. During the last mile, maintain your pace or slow down; do not sprint the last part of the race unless you have practiced this in your training. Run/walk as you train.

Appendix B

IMMDA ADVISORY STATEMENT ON CHILDREN AND MARATHONING: HOW YOUNG IS TOO YOUNG?

This paper and statement were prepared for IMMDA by:
Stephen G. Rice, M.D., Ph.D., M.P.H., FAAP, FACSM
Program Director, Sports Medicine Fellowship, Jersey Shore
Medical Center, Neptune, New Jersey; Clinical Associate
Professor of Pediatrics, University of Medicine and Dentistry of
New Jersey–Robert Wood Johnson Medical School, New Brunswick,
New Jersey;
and Susan Waniewski, M.D.
Fellow in Sports Medicine, Jersey Shore Medical Center, Neptune,
New Jersey.

This statement was unanimously approved at the IMMDA
General Assembly, Fall 2001.
This paper was editorially prepared for publication by an
IMMDA committee of Drs.; Steve Van Camp, M.D.,
FACSM (Chair), Lewis G. Maharam, M.D., FACSM;
Pedro Pujol, M.D., FACSM; and Jan Thorsall, M.D.

ADVISORY STATEMENT: Marathon running should be reserved only for those individuals who have reached their eighteenth birthday.

Introduction

Over the past dozen years, the world has witnessed, with accelerated speed, the erosion of children experiencing and enjoying childhood and adolescence. There has been a drive to have children grow up quickly and become immersed in the adult world, where they will spend the vast majority of their years. This is done in virtually every phase of their young lives, often by caring parents and communities, without a true understanding of the developmental and emotional needs of childhood and adolescence.

Justification for such thinking comes from the notion that "Life is competitive, life is 'a race.' We must start early on that path to ultimate success." Examples of such misconceptions, myths and inappropriate expectations begin almost from birth, progress through infancy and early childhood, and culminate in adolescence. They are seen in areas of learning, eating and physical activity. And so it is with the notion that running a marathon race of 26.2 miles is a sensible and appropriate activity for those youngsters less than eighteen years of age.

Children are not small adults. Their anatomy and physiology are developing and not fully mature. Despite these concepts which are intuitively understood in the broadest sense, in practice, and especially in athletic pursuits, these distinctions are forgotten or ignored.

The focus of discussion for some may be exclusively about whether participating in marathon events is detrimental physically to participants. This statement, however, will review the medical literature also in regard to whether there are emotional and developmental issues which should also play a major role in determining the policy regarding young athletes running in full length marathons.

Background

The American Academy of Pediatrics Committee on Sports Medicine and Fitness has published various statements in recent years regarding reasonable guidelines for youth participation in physical activity. One such statement published by the American Academy of Pediatrics (AAP) in May 2000 addresses the benefits of physical fitness and activity in schools (1). The key point of this statement is that positive health related behaviors acquired in childhood are more likely to be carried into adulthood (1, 2, 3). Thus, aerobic distance running for fitness as a child can clearly be beneficial to one's health as an adult (1, 4). However, such fitness can be attained without ever approaching the rigors of training and distance covered in preparing for and running in marathons (5).

In another such statement in June 2001 titled "Organized Sports for Children and Preadolescents," the AAP committee outlines clear recommendations for childhood involvement in organized sports (6). The overall suggestion is to set reasonable goals for the child including acquire basic motor skills, increase physical activity levels, learn social skills to work as a team, learn good sportsmanship and have fun. One could contend that marathon participation could meet many of these goals. However, in this same statement, the AAP committee implies that sporting activity should be geared to meet the developmental level of children and adolescents in regard to their physical abilities, cognitive capacities, initiative and interest (6, 7). This is not possible for a child marathoner. Emotional burnout is a real phenomenon that can have the exact opposite effect of that intended by participation. Children may develop feelings of failure and frustration when the demands, both physical and cognitive, exceed their internal resources.

Yet another statement published by the AAP in July 2000 addresses intensive training and sports specialization in young athletes (8). This statement warns against early specialization due to negative psychological effects. Most athletes report elite level competition to be a positive experience, but early specialization leads to less consistent performance, more injuries, and shortened sports careers than those who specialize after puberty (8, 9).

In their statement on *triathlon* participation by children in 1996, the AAP Committee on Sports Medicine and Fitness recognizes that children younger than 18 years require shorter distances of competition and specific guidelines to protect children from harm in competitions designed for adults (10). The AAP statement clearly delineates safety precautions to be followed in designing such a competition. Their recommendations state that triathlons for children and adolescents, like all other activities, should be specifically designed to meet their needs and provide "safety, fun and fitness rather than competition." The distances for each of the three events are significantly below those used by adults; further, there are distance categories for those aged 7 to 10; those aged 11 to 15, and those aged 15 to 19. The AAP statement outlines safety guidelines, including: tapering events in accordance with weather conditions, requiring a pre-event swim test, requiring an appropriate number of lifeguards for the swim, holding the swim in pools of appropriate temperature water rather than in open waters, closing off the bicycle course to motor vehicles, mandating bicycle helmet use, providing adequate fluids during and after competition, preparing to handle medical problems or emergencies, and screening all athletes prior to competition (10). These recommendations underscore the concept that it is appropriate and necessary to provide clear guidelines and modifications for participation by a child in an "adult" event.

A clear-cut physical barrier to marathon running in children is the decreased ability to withstand climatic heat stress by the exercising child or adolescent (11, 12, 13). The data (enumerated in a 2000 AAP Sports Medicine and Fitness Committee statement) show that children do not adapt to heat stress as well as adults for several reasons. Children have a greater body surface area to body mass ratio than adults (11, 14); therefore, children gain more radiant heat on a hot day and lose more heat to the surrounding environment on a cool day compared to adults. Children also produce more metabolic heat per unit of body mass, and have a lower sweating capacity, resulting in a decreased ability to dissipate metabolic heat (12, 15, 16). A child takes longer to acclimatize to heat than the adult (11). Finally, the capacity to convey body heat by blood from the body core to the skin is reduced in the exercising child. Thus children are subject to a greater increase in core temperature during endurance activities than are adults.

Overuse Injuries

Long distance running places high mechanical loads on the skeleton, both from ground reactive forces associated with gravity and muscle contractions. While walking, an individual is confronted with a ground reactive force equal to one's body weight. While running, however, these gravitational forces increase to between three and six times body weight, depending on whether one runs on flat surfaces or hilly terrain and also on the length of one's stride (especially when going downhill). A runner will land on each leg between 500 and 1,000 times per mile, again depending on stride length.

The majority of injuries suffered by marathon runners are overuse injuries (17, 18, 19). It is well established that overuse injuries are of multi-factorial etiology, and many of these common risk factors for overuse injuries exist among both children and adults.

Risk factors unique to the growing child are numerous. It is well known that stress fractures, a distinct overuse injury, are a function of the number of repetitions and amount of applied force per repetition (17). Clearly, a child with shorter stride length subjects himself to more repetitions of impact to cover the same distance as an adult. . . .

For the safety of young runners, it is imperative that the training program and its progression be followed closely and monitored carefully. From injury surveillance data conducted on high school athletes in Seattle over a fifteen year period, the activity with the highest rate of injuries was girls cross-country; this injury rate was statistically significantly higher than the other known "high risk sports" of football, wrestling and gymnastics (20, 21, 22, 23). Boys cross-country also had a surprisingly high rate of injuries, placing fifth overall (behind girls cross-country, football, wrestling and girls soccer). Distance running among adolescent boys and girls is thus associated with a relatively high rate of injury. For these athletes, the competitive distance is no more than 3 miles (21, 22, 23). Thus, training to run in a marathon, which is more than eight times the usual cross-country competitive racing distance, is an inappropriate activity for young persons.

Newspaper articles about injuries in cross country running sprouted up after the Seattle high school injury surveillance study was publicized in the lay press (20). Several of these featured stories about injuries to young promising cross country runners, whose careers were cut short because of recurrent significant overuse injuries. Among orthopedic surgeons, some have expressed concern that athletes encouraged to do intensive running prior to skeletal maturity may be predisposed to degenerative diseases of the joints and cartilage as adults (24).

Thus among young athletes, preparing for a marathon is ill advised. In this population, more is not better; there is ample time to increase one's mileage and personal goals when athletes begin college competition at approximately age eighteen.

Psychological Considerations

Many athletes involved in intensive athletic endeavors (which by its very nature marathon participation is) experience emotional burnout and loss of self-esteem, losing interest in the very activity that dominated their childhood and early adolescent years.

Much attention has been given to the issue of psychological effects of marathon running on child participants in the lay press. NBC Nightly News profiled a family during a summer 1988 broadcast (25), with five children (ages 6–16 years), all of whom participate in distance running, with training that includes running seven days per week. This family has been often used in the lay press in arguments for and against youth participation in marathons (26, 27). Reports of this family and other families claim that the running regimen is the child's idea, and that each child truly enjoys this activity. Society, however, accepts the concept that below certain ages, a child is incapable of giving true consent. Heretofore, races have been "sanctioning" these activities by allowing children to compete in marathons, thus providing an avenue of encouragement for this behavior. The fact that marathon record times for children in age groups below 10 and between 10 and 13 exist only serve to fuel the desire to compete and better that record. Marathon running is a serious activity, one that is generally recognized as stressful to all who engage in it. Subjecting children to the stresses of marathon running and training is not healthful.

Female Athlete Triad

Participation in certain sports predisposes female athletes to developing the female athlete triad (28). This triad consists of three interrelated conditions: disordered eating, amenorrhea, and osteoporosis, and is directly associated with intense athletic training (29, 30, 31). Sports which place athletes at higher risk of developing this condition include those in which: (a) thinness is emphasized, such as gymnastics, figure skating, diving, synchronized swimming and ballet; (b) those in which leanness is believed to improve performance, such as long distance running, swimming and cross country skiing; and (c) those in which weight classification exists, such as wrestling, martial arts and rowing (28). Marathon participation clearly is an activity which can lead to the female athlete triad.

Approaches of Other Organizations

The sport of tennis confronted similar issues during the mid-1990s regarding the age at which athletes should be allowed to compete in tournaments. Such regulations were initiated because of the burnout problems of Jennifer Capriati and the impending rise of Venus and Serena Williams. The USATF [USA Track & Field] limited the ages and number of tournaments the participants could engage in. The results have been quite positive. Jennifer Capriati personally shook off her "lost years" to return to championship form and the Williams sisters, forced to conform to restricted opportunities as children, are now the dominant forces in the women's tennis game today. The actions of the USATF were implemented after seeking expert medical opinions regarding the physical, mental and developmental nature of potential problems associated with unrestricted competition by young girls.

Conclusion

Adults and parents are often called upon in our society to set limits and guidelines for precocious and demanding children. It is in the overall best interests of our children to make participation in a full marathon an adult activity, reserved only for those 18 years of age and above. Ample number of opportunities exist after eighteen years of age to participate in this exhilarating experience of marathon running.

While it is conceivable that given proper biomechanics and anatomy, a quality progressive training program, and appropriate maturity and cognitive level, a long distance runner can have a positive experience from participating in marathons prior to eighteen years of age. This special individual would be the exception and not the rule. Examples of such individuals do exist, but serve to demonstrate that decisions rendered regarding participation are not designed with the "exception to the rule" as the critical parameter.

References

1. American Academy of Pediatrics, Committee on Sports Medicine and Fitness and Committee on School Health. Physical Fitness and Activity in Schools. *Pediatrics* 105: 1156–57, 2000.

2. Centers for Disease Control and Prevention. Guidelines for school and community programs to promote lifelong physical activity among young people. *MMWR* (Morbidity Mortality Weekly Report) 46(RR-6): 1–36, 1997.

3. Sallis JF, ed. Physical activity guidelines for adolescents. *Pediatric Exercise Science* 6 (special issue) 299–463, 1994.

4. Mandigout S, Lecoq AM, Courteix D, Guenon P, and Obert P. Effect of Gender in Response to an Aerobic Training Programme in Prepubertal Children. *Acta Paediatrica* 90: 9–15, 2001.

5. Abe D, Yanagawa K, Yamanobe K, Tamura K. Assessment of middle-distance running performance in sub-elite young runners using energy cost of running. *Eur J Appl Physiol* 77: 320–325, 1998.

6. American Academy of Pediatrics, Committee on Sports Medicine and Fitness and Committee on School Health. Organized Sports for Children and Preadolescents. *Pediatrics* 107: 1459–61, 2001.

7. Martens R., Seefeldt V, eds. *Guidelines for Children's Sports.* Reston, VA: National Association for Sport and Physical Education (NASPE): 1–47, 1979.

8. American Academy of Pediatrics, Committee on Sports Medicine and Fitness. Intensive Training and Sports Specialization in Young Athletes. *Pediatrics* 106: 154–157, 2000.

9. Bompa T. *From Childhood to Champion Athlete.* Toronto, Canada: Veritas Publishing, Inc; 1995.

10. American Academy of Pediatrics, Committee on Sports Medicine and Fitness. Triathlon Participation by Children and Adolescents. *Pediatrics* 98: 511–512, 1996.

11. American Academy of Pediatrics, Committee on Sports Medicine and Fitness. Climatic Heat Stress and the Exercising Child and Adolescent. *Pediatrics* 106: 158–159, 2000.

12. Bar-Or O. Temperature regulation during exercise in children and adolescents. *Perspectives in Exercise Sciences and Sports Medicine, II. Youth, Exercise and Sport.* Indianapolis, IN: Benchmark Press; 1989: 335–367.

13. Wagner JA, Robinson S, Tzankoff SP, et al. Heat tolerance and acclimatization to work in the heat in relation to age. *J Appl Physiol* 33: 616–622, 1972.

14. Astrand PO. Experimental Studies of Physical Working Capacity in Relation to Sex and Age. Copenhagen, Denmark: Munksgaard: 1952.

15. Haymes EM, McCormick RJ, Buskirk ER. Heat tolerance of exercising lean and obese prepubertal boys. *J Appl Physiol* 39: 457–461, 1975.

16. Drinkwater BL, Kupprat IC, Denton, JE, et al. Response of prepubertal girls and college women to work in the heat. *J Appl Physiol* 43: 1046–53, 1977.

17. Bennell K, Malcolm S, Thomas S, Wark J, and Brukner P. The Incidence and Distribution of Stress Fractures in Competitive Track and Field Athletes. *American Journal of Sports Medicine* 24: 211–217, 1996.

18. Lysholm J, and Wiklander J. Injuries in Runners. *American Journal of Sports Medicine* 15: 168–171, 1987.

19. Macintyre JG, Taunton JE, Clement DB, Lloyd-Smith DR, McKenzie DC, and Morrell RW. Running Injuries: A Clinical Study of 4,173 Cases. *Clinical Journal of Sport Medicine* 1: 81–87, 1991.

20. Bloom M "Girls' Cross-Country Taking A Heavy Toll, Study Shows". *The New York Times*. December 4, 1993, pages 1 and 34.

21. Rice, SG. Development of an Injury Surveillance System: Results from aLongitudinal Study of High School Athletes. *Safety in Ice Hockey Third Volume*. Philadelphia, USA: ASTM. STP1341: 3–18, 2000.

22. Rauh MJ, Margherita AJ, Rice Stephen G. Rice, M.D., Koepsell TD, and Rivara FP. High School Cross Country Running Injuries: A Longitudinal Study. *Clinical Journal of Sport Medicine* 10: 110–116, 2000.

23. Rice, SG. Risks of Injury During Sports Participation. *Care of the Young Athlete*. American Academy of Orthopaedic Surgeons/American Academy of Pediatrics. Rosemont, Illinois, 2000, pages 9–18.

24. Ireland, ML in Stahl L "Running at Risk", *The Courier-Journal*, Louisville, Kentucky, January 4, 1994, pages H1 and H4.

25. NBC Nightly News. Summer 1988.

26. Henderson, T. Is running the right step for kids? *Detroit News*, January 4, 1999.

27. Faigenbaum, A. Physical Activity for Youth: Tips for Keeping Kids Healthy and Fit. *American College of Sports Medicine Fit Society Page*. April-June 2001: 3–4.

28. American Academy of Pediatrics, Committee on Sports Medicine and Fitness. Medical Concerns in the Female Athlete. *Pediatrics* 106: 610–613, 2000.

29. Hobart J. The Female Athlete Triad. *American Family Physician* 61: 2257–64, 2000.

30. Nattiv A. The Female Athlete Triad. *Clinics in Sports Medicine* 13: 405–17, 1994.

31. Putukian M. The Female Athlete Triad. *Clinics in Sports Medicine* 17: 675–96, 1998.

Appendix C

IMMDA'S REVISED FLUID RECOMMENDATIONS FOR RUNNERS AND WALKERS

Writing committee: Lewis G. Maharam, MD, FACSM (chair), Tamara Hew, DPM, Arthur Siegel, MD, Marv Adner, MD, Bruce Adams, MD, and Pedro Pujol, MD, FACSM

Approved by IMMDA: May 6, 2006. Barcelona, Spain

As Medical Directors (IMMDA: International Marathon Medical Directors Association) of the world's largest marathons and endurance events, it is our desire to educate and ensure that our participants consume proper fluids and amounts of fluids during endurance events to remain healthy and perform well. Too much or too little may bring about health concerns and/or poor performance. We therefore offer the following guidance for runners and walkers at all levels to follow in their training and competitive events.

What should you drink? The evidence on this is clear. If your event or workout is longer than 30 minutes you should be drinking a sports drink. The added carbohydrate and electrolytes speed absorption of fluids and have the added benefit of energy fuel and electrolytes. There is actually decreased benefit to watering down or diluting sports drinks or alternating sports drinks with water.

How much should you drink? Drinking too much or too little can be of risk to health and performance. Hyponatremia (low blood salt level due to abnormal fluid retention from overdrinking) and dehydration (due to net fluid losses from under drinking) are conditions easily averted by understanding your individual body needs. Just as you have a unique face and fingerprint, your body's need for fluid is individual as well. Body weight, gender, climate, sweat rate are just a few variables that individualize your needs. It is normal to lose a small amount of bodyweight during a marathon race; bodyweight will re-equilibrate over the next 24 hours through the consumption of sodium and fluids with meals. A weight loss of more than 2 percent or any weight gain are warning signs that justify immediate medical consultation and indicate that you are drinking improperly.

We offer the following ideas and guidelines for you to consider as you assess your individual fluids:

Try to drink to thirst. This advice seems way too simple to be true; however, physiologically the new scientific evidence says that thirst will actually protect athletes from the hazards of both over and underdrinking by providing real time feedback on internal fluid balance. If you are *not* thirsty, try to refrain from drinking. Do not feel compelled to drink at every fluid station nor follow the cues of other runners: their fluid needs are probably very different from your own. If you are "over-thinking" and feel you cannot rely on this new way of thinking, experiment in your training with one of these other ways realizing each has its own cautions as well.

Approximation of Fluid Replacement*

*The reader should understand that there are individual variations: "one size does not fit all." We endorse thirst as the best scientifically supported method for you to use. These alternate methods may not take into account changes in ambient conditions, running speed and terrain which can all change dynamically which thirst as a method to use does.

Runners and walkers who are interested in the endurance "experience" rather than pursuing a "personal best" performance must resist the tendency to over drink. Runners/walkers planning to spend between 4 to 6 hours or longer on the course are at risk for developing fluid-overload hyponatremia and usually do not need to ingest more than one cup (3–6 oz: 3 oz if you weigh approximately 100 lbs and 6 oz if you weigh approximately 200 lbs) of fluid per mile. Athletes should avoid weight gain during an event.

Some participants may find that adjusting their intake to pace or time is easier for them as shown below but remembering thirst is the best method:

Adjust the rate of fluid intake to race pace: slower race pace = slower drinking rate; maximum intake of 500 ml/hr (4–6 oz every 20 min) for runners with greater than 5 hour finishing times (10–11

Table C.1 Recommended Fluid Intake

Finish Time Race Pace	Fluid Intake Rate	Fluid Intake Total
< 4 hr. < 8 min./mile	10–12 oz/20 min. 30–36 oz/hr. 1,000–1,250 ml/hr.	3.4–4.0 liters
4–5 hr. 9–10 min./mile	8 oz/20 min. 24 oz/hr. 750 ml/hr.	3.0–3.5 liters
> 5 hr. > 10 min./mile	4–6 oz/20 min. 18 oz/hr. 500–600 ml/hr.	2.5–3.0 liters

min/mile pace). Weight monitoring is also important: if you gain weight during your workout or event, you are drinking too much!

For a more highly motivated runner/walker who desires a numeric "range," a fluid calculator can provide an estimate of body fluid losses as a generalized strategy for fluid replacement. Participants concerned about peak performance are advised to understand their individualized fluid needs through use of this fluid calculator but always defer to physiologic cues to increase fluid intake (thirst, concentrated dark urine, weight loss) or decrease fluid consumption (dilute or clear urination, bloating, weight gain) while participating. It is also important to recognize that if you use this method in one climate and then travel to a different climate for your event, the humidity will change your sweat rate and therefore your fluid needs.

Fluid calculator: to calculate sweat rate, runners/walkers should follow these steps:

1. Weigh nude before the run.
2. Run/walk at race pace for one hour. (One hour is recommended to get a reliable representation of sweat rate expected in an endurance event.)
3. Track fluid intake during the run or walk; measure in ounces.
4. Record nude weight after the run/walk. Subtract from starting weight. Convert the difference in body weight to ounces.

5. To determine hourly sweat rate, add to this value the volume of fluid consumed (in Step 3).

6. To determine how much to drink every 15 minutes, divide the hourly sweat rate by 4. This becomes the guideline for fluid intake every 15 minutes of a run.

7. Note the environmental conditions on this day and repeat the measurements on another day when the environmental conditions are different. This will give you an idea of how different conditions affect your sweat rate.

Good luck in your training. Experimenting with your fluids can be a fun exercise. Keep in mind that the consumption of beverages and foods containing sodium or carbohydrate should be guided by the goal to minimize loss of body weight and prevent weight gain.

The International Marathon Medical Directors Association (IMMDA) was formed as the Consulting Medical Committee of the Association of International Marathons (AIMS). AIMS is a global organization of marathons and distance races, formed in May 1982. The purpose of AIMS is to (i) foster and promote distance running throughout the world, (ii) work with the International Association of Athletics Federations (IAAF) as the sport's world governing body on all matters relating to road running, and (iii) exchange information, knowledge, and expertise among its member events. AIMS' current roster numbers approximately 300 events which are conducted in more than 90 countries and all seven continents, and among which are some of the world's largest and most prestigious marathons.

The purpose of IMMDA is to (i) promote and study the health of long distance runners, (ii) promote research into the cause and treatment of running injuries, (iii) prevent the occurrence of injuries during mass participation runs, (iv) offer guidelines for the provision of uniform marathon medical services throughout the world, and (v) promote a close working relationship between race and medical directors in achieving the above four goals.

For further information, please contact Lewis G. Maharam, MD, FACSM, Chairman, IMMDA Board of Governors at 24 West 57th Street, Suite 509, New York, NY 10019, 212-765-5763, nysportsmd@aol.com.

Index

About the Author

Lewis G. Maharam, MD, FACSM (Fellow, American College of Sports Medicine), is a primary care sports medicine specialist in private practice at 24 West 57th Street in New York City. One of the most extensively credentialed and well-known experts in the country in the fields of health, fitness, injury prevention, and treatment of athletes and other active people, Dr. Maharam is past president of the Greater New York Regional Chapter of the American College of Sports Medicine and past chair of sports medicine at the former Downtown Athletic Club ("the Home of the Heisman Trophy"). He has served as the medical director of New York Road Runners and the ING New York City Marathon, and is currently the medical director for the Rock 'n' Roll Marathon series. He also serves as chairman of the Board of Governors of the International Marathon Medical Directors Association as well as national medical director for the Leukemia & Lymphoma Society's Team in Training program. Dr. Maharam was appointed USA team physician in track and field for the 1999 World Indoor Championships in Japan. He previously served as USA team physician for the USA Jr. Track and Field team that won the IAAF Championships in Sydney in 1996.

Dr. Maharam writes the "Ask Running Doc" column on Competitor.com (http://runningdoc.competitor.com). He is the author of *A Healthy Back* (Owl Books, 1998), *Backs in Motion* (Henry Holt, 1996), *The Exercise High* (Fawcett Columbine/Ballantine Books, 1994), and *Maharam's Curve: The Exercise High—How to Get It, How to Keep It* (Norton, 1992). Dr. Maharam is an enthusiastic advocate of exercise as not just something we "ought" to do for our health, but something we owe ourselves—something we must do to fully enjoy our day-to-day lives. His award-winning running medicine research has been presented in continuing education seminars for doctors and at numerous speaking engagements aimed at educating the public. His groundbreaking program for preventing and relieving back pain has made Dr. Maharam a sought-after speaker at community group gatherings, and his positive, clear, and witty conversational style has resulted in many TV and radio interviews. He was a frequent guest on *America's Talking Network: Alive and Wellness Show*, and he has appeared nationally on *World News Tonight, Today, Good Morning America, Inside Edition*, CNN, and Fox News as well as CBS talk radio and WFAN. He has traveled the country appearing on local TV newscasts and radio, appearing with sports reporters as well as health and fitness correspondents talking about current issues.

Dr. Maharam graduated Magna Cum Laude from Lafayette College and earned his medical degree at Emory University prior to surgical and medical internships at, respectively, Columbia-Presbyterian Medical Center and Danbury Hospital, an affiliate of the Yale University School of Medicine. After his residency in internal medicine, Dr. Maharam was awarded one of the few fellowships in the new specialty of primary care sports medicine at Pascack Valley Hospital, Department of Sports Medicine.

An expert on staying free of injuries that can afflict athletes and nonathletes alike, Dr. Maharam writes for *Competitor* magazine, competitor.com, newspapers, newsletters, and many magazines. He is frequently sought as a source of medical advice by writers for *Sports Illustrated, Runner's World, Fitness, Self, Shape, Redbook, Time, Newsweek*, the *New York Times, USA Today*, the *New York Daily News, Newsday, Condé Nast Sports for Women, Glamour, Cosmopolitan, Jane, American Health for Women, Men's Journal, Walking, Woman's Day, McCall's, Reader's Digest*, the *New York Post, Allure, U.S. News and World Report, Cooking Light, Women's Sports and Fitness*, and other publications both here and abroad.

With boundless enthusiasm for debunking health myths while sharing the latest discoveries that can help his audiences enjoy longer, more robust lives, Dr. Maharam speaks on topics such as the following:

Marathon Medical Tips. How do you prepare for marathon day? Training tips, injury prevention, dealing with injury, nutritional tips, carbo-loading. Know what to do to finish the 26.2 miles strong and healthy!

Illegal Substances in Sports. It's gone well beyond professional wrestlers and their steroids. From the junior high school student up, competition is tough and the drive to win medals—or just look better—is strong. Dr. Maharam's information and nonconfrontational style have been a success with students, athletes (professional, college, high school, recreational, and weekend), parents, and coaches. He discusses who's using what and why and what everyone should be on the lookout for.

Back Pain? Don't Just Sit There. A program that takes aim at this ubiquitous ailment not by telling people to be quiet and be careful but by telling them to be active and *move!*

Sex and Back Pain. Everyone who has back pain is afraid to ask the question "Can I do it?" Dr. Maharam talks about how one can, male or female, depending on who is having the pain and why!

Making Exercise a Part of Your Life. Why do so many people start an exercise program and quit? Because it's like bad-tasting medicine: good for you but too tough to swallow. They don't know how to get into the exercise feel-good zone that makes people lifetime converts. But it's not hard. Many people after just one lecture have gotten onto the path of lifetime exercise!

Don't Fall into the Mouse Trap. Sitting at a computer doesn't need to cause wrist and back pain. Dr. Maharam's program gives corporate employees a plan for pain-free computer work.

Healthy People. The CPC and ACSM's latest findings on how much exercise you really need for good health and lower cardiac risk. Plus, how easy it can be to eat right without being a scientist or mathematician.

Sports Shouldn't Hurt. Problems like tennis elbow or runner's knee derail more fitness programs than boredom or lack of time ever could. But they don't have to. The secret is being prepared, whether it's for summer biking, tennis, or golf or wintertime skiing. What people need is a season-by-season program that fine-tunes the body for the sports to come.

Exercise: The Best Stress Reducer. People think they need meditation, drugs, or long vacations to deal with the daily tensions of life. There's plenty of medical evidence suggesting what they really need is regular exercise.

Dance Fever. Dance is a sport. Prepare your body for that night out or your everyday workout.

Food as Fuel. Most nutrition-conscious people try to eat right simply so that they can stay healthy. What about eating to get strong, have more energy, and feel better? Sports medicine knows how you can, and it knows that you never have to count a calorie.

The Superman Syndrome. Adolescent athletes think they can go out on the field, play hard at any game they want, and not get hurt. They think they're unbreakable. Not so. But if they prepare, just like adults should, they'll be headed for an active lifetime of good health. Prepare or beware: the most important exercises, stretches, and other conditioning practices "supermen" and "superwomen" should know so that they stay as durable as they feel.

Women in Sports: Yes, They're Different from Men. Female athletes have more to think about than winning. For example, on a typical high school cross-country women's team, 2 out of 10 runners will show evidence of an eating disorder. We're finally beginning to learn some fascinating things about issues like anorexia and bulimia, exercise and menopause, osteoporosis, and hormonal balances. Who's at risk, and what can they do about it?

What Makes the Older Athlete Different? In most sports they're called *masters*. They're ordinary people over 35, and as a group they could beat most 20-year-olds of a couple of generations ago. Why? The body doesn't age the way we once thought it did. We just have to keep it tuned up a little differently as the years go by.

Are You Fit or Just an Athlete? Most of us confuse prowess on the playing field with fitness and health. You can be a top jock and be in awful shape. And vice versa. If you want to stay healthy, stay fit. Then work on the athletics.